Human Social Development

HUMAN SOCIAL DEVELOPMENT

Psychobiological Roots and Social Consequences

BY

DOROTHY R. BLITSTEN

COLLEGE & UNIVERSITY PRESS · *Publishers*

NEW HAVEN, CONN.

To Professor Theodore Abel
Who Provided Opportunity In Abundance

Foreword

I take more than ordinary pleasure in writing a foreword and thus helping to welcome this splendid book. In the first place the book is concerned, from beginning to end, with one of the most important problems in contemporary sociology and social psychology, as well as in education and other disciplines. And in the second place it would be hard to imagine any scholar better qualified than Dr. Blitsten for approaching the problem.

The problem I speak of is that contained in the book's title: *Human Social Development*. In whatever terms the problem is expressed in ongoing research and teaching today it is plainly a very fundamental one. I see no reason for repeating here what the author has set forth so eloquently herself in the Introduction. It will suffice to note that by "human social development" Dr. Blitsten means a good deal more than mental development alone; and obviously much more than physiological development—though both mental and physiological states are clearly involved. Equally important—especially to those of us who work from structural points of view in our approach to the social bond—is the reminder Dr. Blitsten gives us that her perspective of human social development is a great deal more than what is commonly implied by such phrases as "internalization of social norms" or "learning process."

I can think of no better way of giving substance to the author's guiding perspective in the book than through a few words taken from her own text. When we speak of human social development we are referring directly and precisely to the important fact that the psychobiological potentialities of human beings depend for their development upon access to social relationships. The potentialities do not create the relationships. The relationships most assuredly do not create either the potentialities or the resulting patterns of human social behavior that we see during all phases of the individual's life.

Particularly important is Dr. Blitsten's emphasis, brilliantly expressed in several crucial sections, upon the period of physical immaturity of the individual. I regard her chapters on the infant, juvenile, and adolescent stages of individual development as by far the best on the subject I have chanced to read anywhere. Writing as one interested foremost in the nature of human interaction and in the character of the social bond, I have gleaned from these chapters a very great deal that I now realize that I needed to know.

But by singling out the first three chapters I do not wish to seem to imply lack of respect for the others in the book—those dealing with the later phases of individual social development. I have learned much from her chapters on the mature and the aging in our population. And the reason is precisely the same as with respect to the earlier chapters. Always the book is concerned with, and able to communicate lucidly to the reader, those subtle but puissant, those microsociological but fully empirical, processes whereby human beings become, and remain, human social beings.

I cannot praise too highly the organization of the book into the several ages of individual social development, from infancy to old age. I know of no superior treatment anywhere of the relation of each of these ages in the individual to appropriate patterns of social interaction, to appropriate social structures, and to social norms. The final chapters in which Dr. Blitsten explores, with great imagination as well as learning, the more general connections between individual social development and the larger social order could, in fact, be read by themselves. But taken as the cumulative products of insights and materials contained in earlier chapters they naturally reach their greatest value to the reader of the entire book.

Finally, a few words on the author. I said above that it would be difficult to imagine anyone better qualified to write this book. She grew up, as she tells us, in an environment steeped in medical and therefore biological learning and insight. She actually attended medical school for two years. When she studied as an undergraduate in sociology and anthropology it was in one of the two or three greatest departments in this area we have thus far had in the United States: that of the University of Chicago in the 1920's. There she could not help coming under the magisterial influence of George Herbert Mead, to this day the preeminent American student of the processes of social and symbolic interaction. And, finally, Dr. Blitsten added to her education in sociology and social psychology the extraordinary insights that came in this country from the great Dr. Harry Stack Sullivan, explorer *nonpareil* of dynamic psychiatry.

Dr. Blitsten has been working, studying, teaching in the area covered by this book for a good many years. It is good that she has written *Human Social Development*, thus reaching far more persons than is possible in class or seminar. I regard this book as a profoundly important contribution to contemporary studies of man and society.

Robert Nisbet

University of California, Riverside

Contents

Chapter   *Page*

I   Introduction   13

II   Infancy   30

III   Childhood   48

IV   Juvenile   69

V   Pre-adolescence   86

VI   Adolescence   101

VII   Social Maturity   125

VIII   Some General Connections between Individual Social Development and Social Organizations: Socialization   164

IX   Some General Connections between Individual Social Development and Social Organizations: Enculturation   192

X   The Mental Foundation of Human Social Life   204

    Bibliographical Background   216

    Index   219

Chapter One

Introduction

HUMAN SOCIAL DEVELOPMENT is not the same thing as mental development. Social development cannot occur in the absence of mental development, but the latter does not guarantee much of the former. It is failure to understand this fact that underlies the frequent bewilderment expressed by people when they discover that learned men, and even therapists, are not infrequently incompetent husbands and fathers, bigoted citizens, and irresponsible colleagues. "How can a man who knows so much, or who is so helpful in solving other people's problems, be so incompetent in handling his own affairs?" they ask. An understanding of some of the specific aspects of social development and of the fact that it is only rather tenuously related to intellectual ability and knowledge goes a long way toward answering the question.

The social development of human beings is not synonymous with either their personality or emotional development. However these are defined, they pertain to highly individual characteristics and states of being. They do not evolve independently of life with other people and they both influence and are influenced by the nature of exchanges between them, but they primarily involve each individual's own processes. Strictly speaking, the personality traits and emotions of individuals can be appraised by others, but not shared. Strictly speaking, they can be responded to and coped with, but not participated in.

Neither is the social development of human beings simply "the internalization of norms" nor the "learning of roles." Clothes do not make the man, nor consciously exercised manners a gentleman. Role-learning does not evoke thought. An actor must be cultivated in the skills of the profession of acting before he can perform the roles he will be called upon to play. Certainly, social development involves the acquisition of ability by individuals to regulate their behavior according to norms that are current for the people among whom they live and to cooperate with particular people to achieve particular ends in particular ways. But their ability to do either depends upon general and basic modifications of their psychobiological resources that result from the general fact that they must live among others and, therefore, make some adaptations to their presence. It also depends upon the general fact that human beings can no more reach competent adulthood without integrating a rather large repertoire of cultural entities into their organic processes than they can survive physically without ingesting and digesting rather large quantities of chemicals. In short, whether or not, or how well, a person can enact a role or maintain a stable relationship or association with others in a variety of complex organizations, depends upon his social development.

What this is, at least in part, and how it is achieved, is the subject of this book. The social development of individuals can be conceptually differentiated from their mental and personal development and from their capacity to perform as social units in particular social organizations despite the fact that all of these are interdependent in life. They are not identical series of events. Social development leads specifically to general abilities that enable individuals to form stable relationships with a variety of other people and to operate with them to achieve common ends in increasingly complex organizations, even when their individual motives for seeking these ends are different. People with strikingly different levels of mental and personal development can manifest the same social abilities. These abilities involve the use of cultural means, some of which must be shared by people who live together if effective cooperation is to occur. Therefore, social development also leads to the integration of a cultural repertoire into the organic equipment of every human being.

The elucidation of the development of capacity for relationship *per se* together with the cultural modification of organic processes, is essentially a sociological interest. It is not a psychologist's or a psychiatrist's inquiry into the nature of the human mind and mental processes or of the integration of experience. It is not concerned with the welfare of individuals. It is concerned with the competence of adult human beings for the initiation and maintenance of social organizations and the cultural accumulation of mankind)

In general, the social development of human beings refers to the fact that their psychobiological potentialities depend for their development upon access to social relationships, social organizations, and cultural phenomena, and that the ability of people to sustain relationships and use a cultural repertoire is an outcome of their subordination by others to both during their years of physical immaturity. The modifications that result are not superficial additions to individual organisms, like frosting on a cake, they are integrated by organic structures and functions. Indeed, the functions of the individual human apparatus for speech and thought cannot be initiated in the absence of experience with other people and culture. These are ingredients in the cake, so to speak. It is this, and not the mere fact that human beings must live collectively, that makes them social animals.

This dependence on people and cultural entities introduces a vast source of variation into the development of human beings to maturity. Differences in biologically given structures and potentials cannot be anything like as great as are the possible differences in experience with other people and access to culture. This is not to say that psychobiological differences do not exist. The misuse of observations about biological differences and the confusion of differences in cultural modification with differences in organic potentiality have made social scientists wary of dealing with biological variation. Besides, there is scarcely any aspect of an adult human being that is socially relevant that is not so modified by his particular experience with people and culture that it is difficult to ascertain what the organic function would be unmodified, if it could function at all.

But, given the psychobiological resources of human beings, the actual realization of these potentialities in every particular human being will be subject, not only or merely to biological growth, but to the selective effects of each individual's actual experience with other people, the ways in which they are related to him or her and to each other, and the particular cultural accumulation used by them. Every structure and function of a human body is modified by this experience and, most important of all, the mental abilities of human beings, which distinguish them from all other living creatures and are responsible for the whole realm of social phenomena are overwhelmingly dependent upon other people and culture for their development, efficiency, and maintenance. It should be remembered that mature adult human life is largely "mentally integrated life," to quote H. S. Sullivan, a fact also implied by George Mead in his title: *Mind, Self, and Society*.

The processes involved in the social development of human beings and the conditions that promote them are both numerous and complex. Furthermore, most of them are not directly accessible to the senses. They must be inferred in large part. What is worse, we are still ignorant about the nature of some factors which we know are of the utmost significance: of mind, for example, and probably, of the very existence of others. But the biological resources of human organisms have been better charted and some of them determine what is socially necessary and what is socially possible. Only the functions and products of the developed and cultivated human mind can greatly transcend individual organisms and these depend upon social modifications of these organisms. And so it is possible, and, in my opinion, useful, to anchor the analysis of human social development to the biological resources that are chiefly involved.

It is the release of these resources through somatic growth and their loss through somatic regression that imposes a pattern of serial stages of growth upon social development. Growth by no means guarantees the social and cultural elaborations of psychobiological potentialities that are manifest as social and cultural attributes and skills, but it makes them possible. For example, no amount of effort can evoke the ability to speak in an infant for many months after birth. A child can memorize the words of *Hamlet*, but no one can convey its meaning to him. It is the appearance of new psychobiological potentialities as manifest abilities that characterizes stages of somatic growth and it is the cluster of social relationships and organizations and cultural tools that these both require and evoke for their peculiarly human cultivation that constitutes the stages of social development for individuals. The social and cultural attributes of individuals result from the interplay of these factors and, therefore, they also appear in serial order.

Because I frequently refer to "potential capacities released through growth" it is necessary to be clear about the meaning of the word *potential*. *Potential* refers to the inference that some trait or ability that is *not* present at a given time may be, or will be, manifest if and when particular factors and conditions are available to release the potential and cultivate the trait. Such inferences are especially valid for instances in which a sequence of events has been repeatedly observed. Thus, many inferences about physical potential for different phases of the life-span of organisms have been well founded.

Potentiality does not refer to a trait or condition that has developed, but happens to be absent at a given time. It is not candy in a box from which the lid can be removed to reveal contents fully formed. Rather, it is the knowledge that someone may have that if certain ingredients are available, are mixed in certain ways, and are heated to certain degrees of temperature for certain periods of time something called candy will appear. Potentiality also includes the availability of essential ingredients. The referents to the word *potential* must include all the necessary factors for the appearance of something as well as what the thing itself contributes to its appearance. The potentiality in human infants for speech includes other people who will pattern their sound-making in particular ways, communication with others to establish validated meanings as referents to words, and the cultural ingredient of an established language, as well as the psychobiological apparatus for it.

The term *potential* is sometimes confused with the term *latent*.[1] *Latency*, in contrast to *potentiality*, does refer to

[1] Robert K. Merton, *Social Theory and Social Structure* (Glencoe, Illinois: The Free Press, 1957), Chapter I.

something that was once manifest, but that is no longer apparent at some given time. This is, I think, the implication of the "latency period" of psychoanalytic formulation in which it is assumed that sexual, or sensual, gratifications openly sought in infancy and the "oedipal phase" are in abeyance for a time and will erupt into action with the onset of puberty. Whether this is a fact or not, the use of the word *latent* refers to the absence of phenomena once manifest and, hence, known to be available for future use, if and when the occasion arises to evoke it.

The use of the words *potential* or *latent* to describe social behavior or effects is ambiguous because our knowledge of determined social sequences is meager. We are much less informed concerning what specific conditions are necessary to produce particular social manifestations than we are about the appearance of physiological capacities. We are confronted with evidence that seems to indicate that different configurations of social conditions produce similar results and that similar configurations produce different social results.

However, the point is that the term *potential* has been borrowed from biology and *latent* from psychology by sociologists and other social scientists and that for them these are difficult concepts and are often of questionable use. Certainly, inference is more conspicuous than established fact when these terms are used by sociologists. *Latent*, as used by Merton in "latent and manifest functions," for example, sometimes refers to *potential*, sometimes to unintended effects, sometimes to something improvised, sometimes to something that has been unnoticed. In short, it is used to cover aspects of social organizations and situations that are not specifically formulated in public rules and norms and goals which may, or may not, have attracted the attention of most participants. The examples given are often of something manifest but unmentioned, a version of "the institutional evasion of institutional rules."

For example, there is the case of the influence of personal friendships on recommendations of clients to colleagues among doctors and lawyers for whom professional skill is presumed to be the only acceptable criterion. In fact, there is nothing "latent" about this practice. Usually, a practitioner believes that his friend is as competent as another, though this may not be the case. However, it is a common practice that is simply not discussed outside of small professional circles.

Enough has been said to suggest caution when either term is encountered. I use the term *potential* solely with reference to the appearance of psychobiological capacities in serial stages of growth, such as capacity for walking, for speech, for reproduction, which are clearly not present at birth and which appear at approximately the same age in everyone in the absence of grave defect or external interference. My purpose in calling attention to these biological developments is that their functional competence and incompetence depends in part upon social conditions and accounts for some of them. The fact that individual psychobiological resources require cultivation by other people and cultural entities is the ultimate basis for the appearance and maintenance of the social and cultural phenomena that are both the outcome of collective human life and the condition for its survival and evolution.

I have found it useful to divide the course of the social development of individuals into eight stages: infancy, childhood, juvenile, pre-adolescent, adolescent, early adulthood, middle age, and old age. The association with stages of somatic growth stems from the fact that the social traits that are typically evolved in each phase depend in part on particular psychobiological resources that characterize given periods of growth and regression. Roughly, the chronological limits of these stages of social development, insofar as growth makes the social development possible are the following: Infancy—birth to 18/24 months; childhood—18/24 months to 5/6 years; juvenile—5/6 years to 8/10 years; pre-adolescent—8/10 years to 12/13 years; adolescent—12/13 years to 18/20 years; early adulthood—18/20 years to approximately 35; middle age—35 years to approximately 55/60 years; old age—60 to death. However, the developments that are my subject are not themselves somatic. Biological growth does not in itself guarantee them, it only makes them possible, and there is no necessary correlation between the physical and social levels of development of any given individual.

Growth assures the attainment of biological maturity for all human beings who are not physically defective. It is difficult even to define social maturity in terms that are independent of particular cultural standards and the skills that are needed for the successful pursuit of satisfactions and security of individuals in particular societies, or parts thereof. Furthermore, whatever the definition, the achievement of the full range of social and cultural acquisitions that it includes is the exceptional accomplishment of a minority of adults in any population. There are adults everywhere whose social development has been arrested at some stage far short of social maturity, however that is defined. There are few adults anywhere who can maintain their maximum level of social competence in all social situations and with all kinds of people.

If social development refers to the cultivation of abilities in individuals that enable them to act as durable and efficient units in collective organizations and, at the same time, manage to satisfy their own needs, one obvious requirement for so doing is their development of an extensive degree of self-regulation of their individual impulses toward absolute satisfactions. Another essential requirement is the acquisition of enough of the cultural entities that are used by the people among whom they live to make cooperation with them possible. The social maturity of an individual may be presumed when he can live comfortably among his kind while he cooperates with some of them to maintain the organizations and institutions that are necessary to them all.

Nevertheless, the conception of social maturity must be open-ended. Dependent as it is on social and cultural circumstances, one would have to conclude that some society known to man had succeeded in providing optimal social and cultural conditions for mankind in order to determine the upper limits of adult social development. There is no evidence to support such a conclusion. Social organizations continue to increase in size and complexity. The cultural store of mankind has been accumulating at increasingly rapid rates and its distribution is expanding far beyond previous limits. Currently, one is tempted to wonder whether or not human biological evolution, which is not apparent to us, but which one hopefully assumes is continuing, can proceed fast enough to adapt humankind to the results of its own capacities. The best we can do at present to indicate upper levels for social development is to describe a range of degrees of self-regulation and cultural inclusiveness which represents the most that some people have achieved and which we may assume, therefore, others could achieve given the same resources and opportunities.

However, some degree of social and cultural development is an essential aspect of the realization of the biologically given pattern of human beings. It has been argued by some that human beings can reach physical maturity without undergoing the social and cultural restrictions and modifications that characterize all observed human life. This is the claim for a "natural man" who, left to his own devices, would be healthy, happy, wise, and good, though he be a "noble savage." Rousseau is the most distinguished advocate of this conception. Edgar Rice Burroughs' Tarzan is, perhaps, its most popular personification. It is a conception rooted in the impulses with which, apparently, all human beings are born, to have what they want, when they want it, the way they want it, regardless of the needs of others.

This condition is most nearly achieved *in utero*. It vanishes with birth and, thereafter, the road toward a comfortable measure of individual satisfaction includes other people whose presence and whose needs must be respectfully attended for the prosperity of all. Altruistic responses toward others are cultivated responses. Nonetheless, they are the only guarantee for individuals whose characteristics compel them to live in stable collective arrangements in order to obtain adequate, though not absolute, satisfactions of their own needs. Although it is obvious that some particular associations and cultural means for their maintenance and use are not only expendable, but may seriously interfere with human well-being, it does not follow that human beings can dispense with all of them. Some are as vital to human survival, development, and maintenance as food and protection against the elements. In my opinion, the following chapters support this conclusion.

I use the device of following an ideal-typical scheme of the stages of social development of individual human beings because it seems to me the best way to organize materials that must be understood in order to explain a number of important *general* and *collective* social phenomena: ethnocentrism, resistance to or acceleration of social change, or the relation of individual social traits to the maintenance of complex organizations, for example. Roughly, the adults in large populations embody all stages of social development. Some are essentially childish in social terms, others juvenile, others adolescent, some have the range of competence that represents social maturity in their societies.

Particular collective performances can be better understood, and perhaps regulated, if the social capacities of the participants can be identified. For example, in an interesting book called *Coup d'Etat* by Edward Littwak, the author discusses ties between ex-colonial countries and their former colonial administrators that mitigate against successful coups: "There are many more countries which are in the gray area between effective independence and total submission. Ex-colonies provide many of these more subtle cases of dependence, and the presence of the former mother country is very real, and very effective. Instead of large and expensive armies there are military and economic advisors, there is economic aid and, *above all, the tight web of long established dependence in non-political areas.*[2] Thus, schooling follows patterns originally established in colonial days. The organization of the professions follows the metropolitan system, and thus is very important where the ruling elite is composed of lawyers whose whole raison d'etre is based on the use of a particular procedure and code of law. Trade is often largely tied to the ex-colonial power because of the hold of inherited tastes, habits (*enculturation*) and the fact that trade links are often based on long established relationships and communication (*socialization*).

"The power of these links between ex-colonies and the former colonial power varies from case to case. But quite unobtrusive ties can sometimes give sufficient leverage to the latter to prevent or oppose a coup."

These "unobtrusive ties" are creating serious complica-

[2] Edward Littwak, *Coup d'Etat* (New York: Alfred E. Knopf, 1968), pp. 28, 29. Italics mine.

tions, political and economic, around the world. In some places legislation is enacted to eliminate them, in others police or military force, in some, all three. These measures will not, indeed, cannot do so. Why they cannot and what it takes to alleviate them can only be understood in terms of the socialization and enculturation of the populations involved. Some general collective phenomena can be better understood if their relation to some universal aspects of the social development of everyone can be identified. I think that they can be. It is to this end that I present the ideal-typical scheme that follows.

The headings of the categories of factors that I will trace for each stage of development are biological resources, levels of conceptual ability, levels of linguistic ability, interpersonal contexts, cultural contexts, and forms-of-interaction.

It is obvious that biological resources must be available before they can be cultivated for social uses. In a sense, modes of conceptualization belong within the general category of psychobiological potentialities. Ability for both speech and conceptual processes is not present at birth. The former appears near the end of the first year of life. The fully developed form of the latter is not available to most individuals much before the eleventh or twelfth year of life. Those individuals for whom it is developed earlier are called prodigious. Speech is transformed into effective language as it becomes connected with advancing mental skill because this involves the association of established meanings to words. Abstract thought in logical progression requires very complex combinations of both symbols and mental processes. Clearly, for some years, growth as well as cultivation is involved in the achievement of the use of language as a fairly precise means of communication and the use of abstract thought as a means of grasping the nature of the universe and ordering experience in very complex ways. Both are the mark of mature adult human beings. But because these abilities, once established, enable individuals greatly to transcend the merely biological processes of their organisms it seems to me that the factors that are involved in the development of these abilities in individuals should be considered in separate categories.

Human beings do not and cannot live with one another in a random way. Their psychobiological characteristics create needs for particular relationships and particular kinds of organizations. The techniques for organizing people in general are more closely related to the kind of creatures they are than is often assumed. Self-regulation is a consequence of direct experience with other people and its extent in any particular individual depends upon particular kinds of relationships and membership in particular kinds of organizations. The transmission of basic cultural ingredients, such as a language and what is called folkways or mores, is usually achieved by them, as well. It is possible to identify some of these necessary relationships and organizations.

Cultural acquisitions modify the organic structures and functions of human individuals. In the case of their linguistic and mental functions, the integration of a cultural repertoire into the apparatus for them is necessary to initiate the functions themselves. The creation, preservation, and transmission of culture to ensuing generations are among the inescapable demands upon the resources of adult individuals if they, their progeny and, indeed, mankind are to persist. Roughly, there is a cluster of cultural rules and tools that has particular significance for each stage of human development. It is the imposition of these clusters by the people who take care of the young that determines some aspects of the functions of their organic structures. It is these clusters that make up a large part of the repertoire of cultural entities that are used by individuals to regulate their activities. They also determine many of their associations with other people. Although they are originally imposed upon them, individuals experience these cultural additions as though they were inherent elements of their organisms. Once acquired, they are difficult to lose or modify. These cultural acquisitions tend to run parallel with the development of abilities for particular relationships and the two influence each other.

Neither the limitation of individual impulses on behalf of the needs of others, nor the cultural elaborations of means to satisfactions are biologically sensible. Both interfere with the direct satisfaction of biological needs which are always thoroughly egocentric. That for each individual the line between felt biological need and its satisfactions must be complicated by the presence of other people and their demands to meet culturally defined conditions before biological satisfaction is provided to prepare them to live among their kind is not remotely apparent to the young and is only dimly apparent to a good many adults. Therefore, the social and cultural development of human beings depends upon coercion.

The absolute dependence for survival and maintenance of young human beings on older ones compels their initial submission. Only extensive self-regulation and the pursuit of satisfactions by means that were once imposed by others removes adult individuals from constant and direct coercions by the people who control access to whatever they need or want. Only the intrinsic significance of some other people to an individual makes the cultural requirements they impose seem anything more than arbitrary interferences with his individual satisfactions.

In *The Nun's Story* by Katherine Hulme, an experienced sister of the religious order, while describing to a group of new candidates the extreme discipline required to become a full-fledged member of the order, says to them: "This is a life against nature." The implied interference with biological impulses may be greater for nuns than for other people, but it is not much greater than it is for people of extensive social development. The necessity for complicating biological processes and limiting biological satisfactions is incumbent on both. The social manifestations that most distinguish human adults from other animals are achieved by a "life against nature," if that is taken to mean the transcendence of raw biological impulses. Each stage of social development is characterized by particular forms of coercion and, by and large, they are exercised universally. We shall consider the most important of them.

The characteristics of particular relationships of people with one another are not only determined by their needs, or the requirements of collective living, or the ends that the participants seek, or by cultural definition. They are also determined by the actual social capacities of the people involved. Exchanges between people occur in different social modes. For example, the relationship between a particular parent and child operates differently when the child is an infant or toddler than it does when he is an adolescent or a middle-aged man, although it may be said to be the same relationship. The differences are not merely in the services rendered. They involve different forms of interaction, and/or a different distribution of their use, because of changes in the levels of social development of the child and, in some cases, of the parent.

The forms of interaction manifest by individuals in their exchanges with one another have been identified by sociologists, but they are often discussed as though they were disembodied forces that can be called forth to impel, or compel, individuals to behave in particular ways with one another. In fact, forms of interaction, such as superordination, subordination, cooperation, *et al.*, represent degrees of self-regulation of individual impulses in response to others and cannot be evoked between particular people unless the ability to manifest them has been cultivated. Responsiveness to other people as something more than instrumental means to satisfactions is lacking at birth and may be almost as lacking at death at a ripe old age. In either case, cooperation in the absence of direct coercion or promise of immediate gratification does not occur.

Until, or unless, individuals are coerced to compromise their demands for absolute satisfaction of egocentric impulses, other people have no personal significance. The word *responsibility*, or *reliability*, depends on the development of capacity for responding to the nature and condition of other people. Forms of interaction represent degrees of this capacity. Ability to manifest them appears in stages and, for the most part, in a particular serial order. The interpersonal relationships that are especially significant for each phase of development cultivate particular forms of interaction in the participants. For the young, progress in the series of forms of interaction is an important indication of move from one level of social competence to another. The serial development of abilities to manifest all major forms of interaction is an essential element of social maturity.

Because the development of everyone, social and otherwise, depends upon and is influenced by their access to physical, chemical, personal, and cultural resources, and because this access is ultimately determined for most people by the societies in which they live, the stages of social development must be envisaged as proceeding within a complex grid made up of relatively stable relationships and organizations, institutions, cultural accumulations, and material resources. The degree of differentiation that exists in their societies between relationships, organizations, and institutions; the amount, kind, and distribution of both culture and material resources available to the populations of which they are a part; and the size and distribution as well as its categorical differentiations and stratifications of populations, are all determining factors for what is possible for individual development.

Few people have access to all that can be available even in small societies that are, in my opinion, better described as tribal communities because their unity depends upon kinship or some cultural orthodoxy, though everyone in these can be said to be directly influenced by their community as a whole. In large complex societies, no individual has access to all the resources of which it is constituted and the influence of the society as a whole on individuals is indirect for the most part. It is mediated to them by the significant people on whom they are dependent for their satisfaction and security and the groups and organizations in which they actually participate.

All schemes of development are conceptual constructs used to organize observed data in accordance with some generalizations based on inferences drawn from them. These schemes always distort reality in some measure. None of the factors and conditions included in them appear as isolated entities in life. They are present in varying degrees, and simultaneously. They influence one another continuously. "Stages" of anything living are not, in fact, clearly separated from each other. They merge. Furthermore, each individual develops unevenly. He may be highly competent in one sphere of living and woefully inept in another. "Stages of development" are ideal-typical arrangements of factors that tend to cluster together with enough statistical

regularity to justify the designation of the cluster as a category of a particular kind, distinguished from other categories of phenomena.

The term _ideal_ does not imply desirability, it merely indicates that the description is a conceptual construct. The
word _typical_ refers to the selections of the particular indi-
viduating traits of the phenomenon from its entire range of
traits, many of which it shares with other phenomena.
These schemes are useful for the identification of classes of
phenomena. Further, if one knows the factors that characterize the class, one knows a good deal about a particular
phenomenon the moment one identifies its appropriate
category. If one recognizes an object as a chair, for example, one is immediately aware of some aspects of its
construction and knows a great deal about its potential
uses. If a human being is identified as a child rather than as
an adolescent, one immediately sorts out a large number of
items from experience as being relevant or irrelevant for
one's behavior toward him. In life, few particular phenomena manifest all of the ideal-typical traits enumerated
for its class. Particular phenomena are usually more and less
typical. Observation of their deviations from the typical are
illuminating in themselves. By directing attention to significant difference, they initiate inquiry and lead to new information.

My own reading of stages of social development is no
less an abstraction than that of others. No actual individual
is fortunate enough in life to encounter all the conditions
and elements he needs for his development or to encounter
those available to him in the right place at the right time.
The social development of real people is often uneven. But
enough people have been observed and the observations
recorded by biologists, psychiatrists, sociologists, anthropologists, historians, and artists to warrant some general
statements about potentialities for social development of
human beings in general and some of the factors and conditions required for their manifestation.

Freudian emphasis on the importance of the earliest
stages of human life has influenced all specialties of the
social sciences. Therefore, it is necessary to emphasize the
fact that all stages of life make important contributions to

the social competence of human beings. Many social scientists, and even psychiatrists and analysts, have abandoned the view that essential individual personal traits are all but fully determined by the end of the first half dozen years of life. But the notion persists and is still taught in some schools and institutes. I do not subscribe to it because it seems to me that there are several important facts against it.

First, although there are always increasing limitations on the degrees of freedom of choice in a developmental series, in the case of human beings, the number of resources available to them increases for a good many years and opportunities for their cultivation may expand throughout a life span. Changes can and do occur. Therapy itself depends upon this possibility. Secondly, there are important resources that are not available in the early phases of life, such as capacity for reproduction or abstract thought, for example. Something new is added and, therefore, new possibilities must be. Thirdly, conceptual ability in adult human beings transcends their organic structures and can modify their functions and performances. Fourthly, human psychobiological resources wane as well as wax and there is a shifting hierarchy of needs in the life of everyone, daily as well as over a life span. In my opinion, the influences of early stages of development may be significantly operative in later ones, but they may not. Later developments can modify, negate, or supplant earlier ones. In any case, each phase of development has characteristics peculiar to it that cannot be fully derived from previous stages, however much or little they are influenced by them.

Chapter Two

Infancy

EVERY HUMAN BEING starts his life totally dominated by compelling biological needs, the satisfaction of which are imperative to his survival. At the same time, he has no resources by means of which he can gratify these needs by his own efforts; he can only crudely indicate that he is experiencing discomfort. Human infants have no capacity for personal relationships with others in the usual sense of the word. They have no means by which they can identify the needs of others or their personal characteristics. Infants respond to tenderness and the satisfaction of their needs, or to the lack of them, not to the persons who supply or fail to supply them, per se. Furthermore, infants have no awareness of the complex physical, social, and cultural environment in which they exist. They respond only to what impinges upon them directly. They are born into a particular physical, social, and cultural milieu, but they are not yet of it, nor will be to any great extent for a long time.

However, their own organisms ordain, and the people responsible for them intend, that they will ultimately make their contribution to the maintenance of the physical, social, and cultural environment in which, as infants, they merely exist. Their own maintenance as adults will depend upon their ability to do so. The initiation of the developments that lead to this end begin with birth.

Infants are possessed of particular psychobiological resources that not only enable other people to begin to modify them in ways that will enable them to participate in the collective arrangements in which they will live as adults, but that guarantee that the other people who must cultivate these resources will be continuously available. In infancy, the resources and the relationships that are of special relevance to social development are few, but they are of great importance for the future of infants.

The significant biological resources of infants are their absolute dependence on adults for their survival, their ability to cry, the satisfaction response, empathy, and capacity to feel anxiety. The absolute dependence of infants and their cry needs no elucidation, their significance will be discussed in connection with their effect upon and use by others.

The satisfaction response is readily identified for anyone who has actually tended an infant. An infant who is dry, warm, and recently fed falls into a state of a kind of yielding relaxation. Momentarily, all his needs are satisfied. This physical indication of his gratification is greatly rewarding to the person who has served him; in fact, it is the only reward that he can provide directly. It tends to evoke in her—it usually is a woman—a matching state of relaxation and pleasure. In her case, the pleasure is satisfaction in giving satisfaction. In the infant's case it is biological satisfaction. But the two mutually reinforce the agreeable state for both. The reinforcement certainly occurs on a subconceptual level for the infant and most of it is conveyed by the same channels for his provider. Between them, they achieve a kind of primitive trust, total and unthinking.

It is clear that if the circumstances surrounding an infant are such that complete satisfaction of any particular need is unlikely and the degree of comfort that flows from the simultaneous gratification of several basic needs at once is improbable, he will not experience what we call the "satisfaction response" and its counterpart will not be evoked in those who attend him. This failure may be due to the lack of physical resources, or to the absence of people predisposed to do more than merely keep him alive: an orphaned infant in the hands of indifferent keepers, for example; or to a mother whose own development is insufficient, or one who is made so anxious by the infant that anxiety and not satisfaction is conveyed along with the biological gratifications provided. In all such instances, the predisposition to expect something desirable from others which is a great help for subsequent relations with others is not evoked. In the case of the association of anxiety with the satisfaction of basic needs, serious interference with the function of organic processes, such as digestion and sleep, is likely and this, of course, complicates the life of an infant throughout its course.

Little is specifically known of what is here called empathy. It is a word used to refer to channels of communication that are both pre-linguistic and pre-conceptual. That such communication occurs is not in doubt. Infants and young children especially can be observed to respond to the states of being of the people who care for them even though they can have no idea, no conscious conception, of what these states are. Other animals sometimes react in the same way.

These are gross reactions that involve the whole organism. They produce restlessness, or apathy, for example, not clearly differentiated, goal-directed activity in either infants or pets. Infants, and other animals, that are not ordinarily feeding problems, may reject food, or regurgitate it, if their feeder is agitated or angry, or in any way unusually motivated at a particular feeding. In short, it is clear that by channels not yet clearly identified, communication of states of being other than their own is transmitted to infants and young children long before the conceptual means for receiving them are developed. It is this kind of communication that is called empathy.

Its fate in adults is obscure. It is doubtful that empathy is completely eliminated in anyone. However, as capacity for the conceptualization of experience evolves and ability for the use of language as a precise means of communication is developed, these tend to replace empathy as an important channel for exchanges between people. Conceptualization and language are so superior to empathy for communication that they eliminate its use for most adults under ordinary circumstances. It is likely that people who are called highly intuitive or who manifest mediumistic capacities are those in whom the paths of empathy remain open. And they seem to be reactivated for people for whom usual linguistic means of communication are cut off, such as prisoners, inmates of hospitals, or the members of religious orders. It is one of the truisms of human life that abilities that are abandoned in favor of more efficient ones are rarely lost. However, infants and young children have no choice. Empathy, whatever this turns out to be, is the means by which some gross aspects of the states of being of the people who provide for them are conveyed to them.

Anxiety is such an important factor in the social development of everyone that a rather long digression is necessary to clarify what it is.

The capacity to feel anxiety is organic. It is often confused with fear. In fact, it is difficult to distinguish between the two because their physical manifestations are the same: an increased pulse rate, sweating, trembling, gastrointestinal disturbances, weakening of muscle control, and so forth. However, both the situations that evoke them and their personal effects are conspicuously different.

Fear seems to be associated with threats to the organism itself, whatever their source. Fear focuses attention on what is feared. One is clearly aware of what one fears. Finally, however much fears may disrupt effective behavior, they can be controlled and regulated in time. People can become accustomed to fear and operate efficiently despite it: for example, soldiers in battle, many people who habitually use airplanes despite their fear of them, people who are afraid of lightning but who work through an electrical storm, and so forth.

Anxiety is quite different. It is evoked, not by threats to the organism, but by threats to one's acceptability by others. In early life acceptability takes the form of receiving attention on which life itself depends. Throughout life, sufficient approval by some others to guarantee this acceptance as a participant in a great variety of collective associations, some of them vital, is essential for both the physical and social integration of everyone. The feeling of anxiety indicates deterioration of psychological and social security.

Anxiety in general is not to be confused with acute states of psychiatric distress, although it is obviously involved in them. Anxiety is no more pathological in itself than pain. Both are signals that something is wrong; the first, in the interpersonal sphere; the second, in the physical sphere. The absence of ability to feel pain is itself pathologic and a great danger to survival. So is the absence of ability to feel anxiety.

In ordinary life pain is manifest as slight pinpricks, acute discomfort of short duration, either as "stabs" of pain when one moves incorrectly or hits a corner of a table, as itches and aches, not as disabling sensation. They are cues for correcting one's physical situation. In ordinary life, anxiety is manifest as embarrassment, shame, humiliation, and, more commonly, as anger and what Harry Stack Sullivan called "selective inattention." The most common acute form of anxiety is "self-consciousness," which, as everyone knows, can be devastating and totally destructive of performance. This differs from "schizophrenic panic," for example, by being of short duration, which implies that its source is identifiable and amenable to rapid alteration in a favorable direction, which is not true of "panic." This possibility for correction characterizes ordinary pain as distinguished from continuing pain that indicates continuing and not readily modified physical pathology.

However, although anxiety is not pathological in itself, like pain, it is necessarily uncomfortable. Indeed it is less tolerable than pain to which one can grow accustomed, as one can to fear, and which one can master. Anxiety, unlike fear, deflects attention from its source. It is more difficult to identify what produces anxiety and therefore harder to alter the condition. Anxiety tends to diffuse to a larger number of factors which surround its source, but which are not inherently part of it. The diffusion itself makes it difficult to locate the source of anxiety. A consequence of these characteristics of anxiety is that whole areas of experience, or types of activity, or categories of relationships become blocked off from effective attention and use. In order to avoid anxiety one avoids the general situations which have come to evoke it and, more often than not, the interpersonal disapproval that generated it in the first place is beyond conceptual formulation, recall, and deliberate modification.

From birth, vital dependence on others invests their "do's" and "don'ts" with something more than Pavlovian associations of satisfaction or dissatisfaction. They become tinged with threat of non-acceptability by others, of uncertainty concerning their willingness to pay attention to oneself and one's needs. In early life, the threat of withdrawal of attention by the people on whom the young depend is panic-making and so they very quickly do what is expected and wanted by their elders, not only to get what they want, but to avoid anxiety.

Everywhere, people who raise children use the evocation of anxiety as a principal means of coercing them to limit their impulses and to pursue their satisfactions in culturally approved ways. Child-rearing proceeds on an anxiety gradient on which approval brings both satisfaction and the feelings of comfort, happiness, and even euphoria, and disapproval leads through discomfort, anxiety and dissatisfaction to panic. The personal traits so engendered in individuals are in part idiosyncratic, reflecting the accidental assortment of personal traits of their training elders, but, in much larger part, they embody the folkways and mores that regulate the performances and relationships of most of the particular people among whom individuals live. People come to want to do what they were long coerced to do and small hints or indications that they are deviating from what is expected by evoking some form of anxiety become enough to move them back on course.

This development, whereby human beings come automatically to direct most of their behavior and affections and thoughts in approved channels, is also correlated with the development of their capacity for conceptualization and their acquisition of a consensually validated cultural repertoire as part of their chief apparatus for organizing experience, namely their equipment for language and thought. But this complex development is both encouraged and inhibited by the evocation of anxiety by the people involved in its cultivation, chiefly in connection with the enculturation of their dependents whose tastes, ideas, beliefs, manners, morals and so forth they expect will match their own. The stabilization of these and the patterning of areas of freedom and constraint for individuals are largely maintained by the fact that what was anxiety-enforced at its inception is likely to be maintained by the evocation of anxiety in the presence of anything significantly different. In time, what was disapproved touches off biological cues that inhibit action in that direction.

Since the particular sets of approval and disapproval that prevail among particular populations and parts thereof vary, their anxiety-enforcement has the social effect of training people for memberships and relationships with people similar to those among whom they were reared, but it excludes comfortable adaptation to people who are different in important social and cultural respects. It slows down and limits the adaptability of people to strangers everywhere. This is the essential basis of ethnocentrism, prejudice, ingroup and out-group tension, and so forth. People who are different evoke anxiety in one another which can be acutely uncomfortable. They remain unaware of the sources of their discomfort so they rationalize it in ways that will bolster their self-esteem. These most frequently take the form of denigrating people who differ from themselves and anxiety is reduced by patterns of avoidance. Where avoidance cannot be achieved, anxiety mounts and is most likely to be transformed into the sentiment of hatred and aggressive and violent behavior. Because the origins of most of this series are sub-conceptual their modification is not easy to achieve.

The anxiety-enforcement of early training determines more than the selection of people with whom individuals can live and with whom they will cooperate. It condemns some of their potential resources to permanent suppression or repression, while it encourages the development of others. It maps the areas of experience that will be relatively open to experimentation and improvisation, and those that will be rigidly proscribed. It determines the subjects that individuals are capable of learning and those that they cannot master, often because of unremembered taboos imposed by the people who raised them.

No one escapes this anxiety-enforced determination of much, if not most, of what each believes is his most personal and individual repertoire of taste, motives, beliefs, convictions, and so forth. Bertrand Russell once remarked that Kant's categorical imperatives turned out to be "What he was taught when young." This is only partly true, but it is true enough to be witty. Imperatives for most of us are what we were taught when young. Harry Stack Sullivan used to say that competent personal maturity required "recovery from one's culture." He was also referring to what we are taught when young. The only escape from it is the development of a high degree of skill for abstract conceptual thought and its application to a review of individual autobiographies. Since this degree of cultivation is not common and since self-investigation itself evokes anxiety, escape is not common.

If the dynamic processes associated with anxiety are not taken into consideration, the development of personal traits and social and cultural competence may seem to be a relatively superficial thing, a learning by rote or learning of the kind associated with the acquisition of information or skill by conceptual effort. Anxiety may, or may not, be involved in these procedures, but social development always involves anxiety because it requires the cultivation or maintenance of basic psychobiological resources by significant other people. They are significant because this is what they do. Therefore, their negative reactions to those they cultivate have the power to set off the biological warning system we call anxiety. This insures the stabilization of desired responses and performances, many of which operate as automatically in human beings as do the merely biologically determined responses of other animals. Since no one can live in a constant state of alertness and everyone needs a cultural repertoire shared by the people with whom he habitually lives, anxiety-enforced social and cultural attributes are useful. They are inadequate and become an impediment to effective living only if and when the social conditions in which people live, or the kind of people with whom they live, are drastically changed.

The disappointing results of many attempts at racial and religious integration are largely due to the anxiety that propinquity evokes in the participants. The experimenters are well intentioned and the initial participants willing, but both overlook the fact that most individuals are acutely uncomfortable with people who manifest different and strange manners, tastes, speech, values, etc. What is sometimes tolerable on occasion and in small doses is not in daily contact. Individuals become "sensitive," take offense at one another's terminology and folk humor, begin to denigrate one another's social traits, accuse one another of ill-will, begin to express open hostility to one another, may become violent, and not infrequently end by demanding separation. There are internal as well as external sources for social discrimination for everyone involved in associations with people who are conspicuously different. It is highly probable that without the compelling biological urge of lust, the so-called "war between the sexes" would be much hotter than it is.

Among people whose social skills enable them to move among people with heterogeneous social traits with considerable ease, the measure of what they have overcome to do so is often apparent in a kind of rapid social census made by them on entering such a mixed gathering. In the United States, for example, the relative number of Jews, Catholics, Protestants, blacks, whites, representatives of particular ethnic enclaves, and so forth, do not go unnoticed by most people in a socially mixed group. These same people do not make similar calculations regarding occupational, income, educational, or, under ordinary circumstances, even political distributions among them. These arrangements are not as anxiety-enforced as are racial and religious affiliations and are, therefore, more easily transcended.

Nevertheless, the capacity to feel anxiety is as necessary to human life as the capacity to feel pain. Neither can be viewed as ends to be sought, they are warning systems: pain for physical threat, anxiety for personal threat. Collective social life depends upon the latter. People who, for reasons unknown, do not suffer anxiety, or who anaesthetize it by taking drugs, for example, cannot participate effectively in collective enterprises. The first are likely to be what psychiatrists call "psychopathic characters" who frequently fall into criminal categories. The second "drop out" of routine collective actions. Excessive pain or anxiety are both disintegrating for human personal organization. The deliberate and unnecessary evocation of either is "torture." But the absence of reliable biological regulators of behavior in human beings makes it vital for them that the social and cultural modifications that are substituted be stabilized. Anxiety seems to be the principal means for so doing.

It is evoked via empathy in infants, often unintentionally. Infants are more likely to be "infected" by the anxieties of the people who tend them than suffused by their own because they cannot differentiate between their mothering ones and their moods with any degree of precision and, therefore, cannot be aware of anything so subtle as social disapproval. This makes anxiety-enforced responses initiated in infancy particularly inaccessible to modification in later life.

Much that characterizes infants and life with them follows from their pre-conceptual and pre-linguistic state. It is the absence of ability to formulate experience in conceptual terms, which is the basis for memory that is open to recall, that accounts for the "amnesia" that obscures infancy and early childhood. The experiences of these early stages of life certainly influence later ones, but in the absence of anyone's ability to remember them precisely, inferences about them and their connections with later events must be based on the observations of adults. Some vestiges from these periods can be identified in the manifestations of later life, even of adulthood. It has been suggested by psychiatrists and psychologists, that the mental processes manifest in dreams and in disorders of neurotic and psychotic adults, and in drug-induced states in which the higher functions of the central nervous system are inhibited, reflect in some degree the psychological activities and condition of infants and children.

On the basis of such observation and inference, it is assumed that infants live in a little differentiated psychological condition. Theirs is a sort of cosmic state of being with their organisms and compelling somatic impulses as its center. There is little distinction between their own organisms and people, things, and events external to them. There is no time, no sequence, no movement of thought to establish connections between people and things other than their direct impact on the states of the infants themselves, which they apparently experience as emanating from themselves. This is not so much a state of egocentricity, since infants seem to make no real distinction between themselves and others experienced as discrete entities, as it is a state of imprisonment within the confines of their bodies. Release from this domination is gradual and depends on physical growth as well as the continuous efforts of some other people to attach their attention to objects, to themselves, and to events.

The cry is the most powerful tool available to infants for communicating their states of being and for influencing the people who tend them. It is crude, but very effective. Most adults in charge of infants respond to their cry with alacrity. It is a sound that easily tyrannizes a household, a fact that generations of infants discover promptly and use to advantage. Crying is the precursor of speech. It uses the same apparatus and serves some of the same basic purposes. The crying of new-born infants is undifferentiated, but it takes very few days before some patterning becomes associated with different conditions. Nurses and mothers soon identify the cry that indicates hunger, the cry that suggests being wet and cold, the cry of emergency, and later, the coo of contentment and the gurgles of play with sounds. This is not essentially different from the sound-making of other pets and the responses of their keepers.

It seems that the differentiation of crying by infants must reflect a growing ability on their part to differentiate states of being. Toward the end of infancy the noise-making involved in crying is further differentiated into the patterns of sound that will later be organized into the particular speech that the adults are transmitting to their young. Certainly accuracy of response by mothering ones, which is attested to by their administration of services that end the crying, reinforces and advances the process of differentiation. But for all of infancy, for much of early childhood, indeed, throughout life to some extent, the use of crying is pure magic.

Infants cry and satisfactions appear. What had made them appear, how they are achieved, are unknown. No connections between the factors that intervene between the cry and its result can be made by infants and young children and frequently are not made by much older people. This magical use of crying is of special importance because the initial words of children are used in the same way. This is a source of considerable confusion for the social development of everyone. For, although none but the most doting parents attribute profound, or even precise, conceptual meaning to an infant's cries, many adults almost automatically attribute it to words, no matter who speaks them. The consequence of this error will be traced later. However, the magical cries of infants are not only instrumental for bringing them what they need, they are potent means for manipulating the people around them.

These particular attributes of human infants determine what can be, and is done for and with them, in large part. Given their state of helplessness and long post-natal immaturity, the only possible relationship to an infant is one of constant attention to its compelling needs. Therefore, the interpersonal relationships of special importance for the stage of infancy can be generalized as mothering. Usually the biological mother is extensively involved in this mothering, but she need not be, and in few instances is she the only one involved. Anyone who handles an infant, as long as he or she wishes it to survive, is reduced to motherhood, in a social sense. The infant's condition leaves no room for choice. As a relationship it is unilateral; that is, infants know nothing of it. For the adults involved, it is usually full of social significance, individual and collective.

Of the total cultural repertoire of mothering ones, which is, of course, a small fraction of the cultural resources available and distributed to the total population in which they live, only some categories are involved in the care of infants. Standard cultural evaluations of the significance of having children and of their "nature" and "rights"; standard evaluations of males and females, of twins, and so forth; standard obstetrical and pediatric practices; prevailing notions about infant-raising; conventions about what constitutes proper food and its preparation, about cleanliness, about hours for sleeping and waking, about body-functions generally; the language spoken by the people on whom infants depend for care, are among the cultural items most relevant to infancy. A not insignificant part of the culture that is introduced into the life of infants is much the same everywhere because infants are so bound to their biological needs that the conditions for their survival do not allow much leeway for essential variation. However, there are countless particular items in each cultural category and many of them have no relevance to biological need. Their sources are other cultural categories, such as religious and political beliefs and doctrines, local economic, educational, and family institutions, and technological development, all of which eventually pertain to the organization and maintenance of collective arrangements rather than to the biological needs of individuals.

To this end mothering ones elaborate the satisfactions they provide their infants with cultural additions: sleeping and feeding schedules, food selection, encouragement or discouragement of movement, amount and kind of physical handling, and so forth—all of which are regularly connected with access to food, sleep, movement, tenderness and such, but are not inherent parts of these requirements. Ultimately, the satisfactions of eating, sleeping, etc. include the cultural additions as an intrinsic condition for satisfaction. Gastro-intestinal systems adjust to particular sequences of ingestion and elimination of wastes and do not function when these are disturbed. They reject some foods. Central nervous systems control alertness, waking, and sleeping, according to the time schedules for work and leisure and sleep that are kept by the majority of people in a population. Bones and muscle grow into particular positions determined by standards regarding posture and motion. The sound-producing potentials of the apparatus for speech are organized for the production of a particular series and combination of sounds. All this, and much more, is begun in infancy. The particular modifications of particular infants depend upon the cultural ingredients added by their particular mothering ones, but no infants anywhere escape cultural modification of some kind.

Total dependence for survival is a massive form of coercion, but it is at the same time a condition that invites coercion as well. It is this dependence that enables mothering ones to manipulate the access of their infants to biological satisfactions and thereby to impose limits on their satisfactions. Their impositions are of two major kinds. The first is the cultural modification just discussed. The second is the social adaptation to the mothering ones themselves.

Mothering ones not only withhold gratifications until some particular cultural condition is fulfilled, but also withhold them until infants stop screaming, or kicking, or pushing their hands or the food container away. It is not long in the life of infants before mothering ones cease to respond to cries identified as cries for attention at times when they intend the infants to sleep or eat. They do respond to well-differentiated cries, and, not much later, are more likely to respond to coos and gurgles with sheer attention. So it is not long before even infants manifest some self-regulation. So do puppies or kittens under similar treatment.

This control of access to the satisfaction of needs is the principal form of coercion used to achieve the social development of infants. It is a conspicuous form of coercion for human beings throughout their lives. How conspicuous it is in later life depends upon the extent of each individual's dependence on others for what they need or want, but since human beings remain interdependent for life almost no one escapes this coercion altogether. Hermits are an exception, but they lead very limited and primitive lives and become odd. Extensive self-regulation reduces the need for coercion by others also and some adults escape a good deal of direct coercion by this means. But infants are not capable of much self-regulation and though they are driven by their biological state to want what they want when they want it, they are in a position that ensures that they get what they want in the form and amount that other people want, and when they want them to have it.

There is another form of coercion exercised on infants by their mothering ones that is made possible by their capacity for receiving some indication of their mothers' states of being through their senses and what we call empathy. Mothering ones register approval and disapproval of the performance of their infants by the increase and decrease of tenderness. Tenderness is, in essence, a willingness to attend to another, to pay attention to him, to supply what he needs, in the case of infants especially, to touch them, fondle them, play with them.

When infants eat well or relax while being handled, or show satisfaction, for example, the voice, the touch, the tension of the skin and muscles, possibly even the smell of their providers, is different from what they are when their infants scream and tense their limbs and refuse food, and so forth. Any young animal is appealing and cuddly in the first instance, and a difficult, frustrating, and even an anxiety-producing annoyance in the second. If the animal is a puppy or a kitten, its caretakers are likely to drop it on the floor. So simple a solution is not available for most mothering ones. The struggle that ensues is usually augmented by the infant's negative response to the negative reactions of the mothering one. It can be reduced if someone takes over who is not irritated by infantile behavior. In any case, the states of mothering ones, positive and negative, are somehow conveyed to infants. Most of them are far more subtle than the one just described and include indications of states that have nothing to do with the infants themselves. For most infants, the promise of tenderness encourages the continuation of whatever they are doing, its decrease discourages it.

The state of infancy limits the mode of any relation with infants to one of superordination and subordination. It takes more social ability than is available to infants to compete or cooperate with others. The extreme subordination of infants to adults is obvious, but the fact that extreme dependency is a powerful form of domination is often overlooked. The extent of its power is amply demonstrated by infants. The birth of a child changes its parents and their relationship to each other and to their friends and relatives forever. The presence of an infant in a household disrupts previous routines and imposes some new ones. For most people, the needs of their infants greatly curtail the immediate satisfaction of many of their own needs and wants, sometimes for years to come. Infants interfere with all kinds of activities of their parents, or other caretakers. In short, the dependency of infants is so great that they are what can be described as a kind of parasite that lives off the social resources and skills of those who wish them to live. Their presence has been known to destroy relationships between spouses and to disintegrate the personal integration of mothers.

Clearly, there is reciprocity between infants and their

mothering ones. If infants are to prosper, their providers must be able to dominate in the long run. But this domination is by no means a simple superordination of the full-grown person over the newly born who are physically helpless and, therefore, in this respect subordinate. Infants have many ways to dominate, not the least of which is their helplessness. The relationship between the young and their elders at the end of infancy is in fact a complex resultant of mutual coercions and satisfactions and dissatisfactions. Although it is true that the significant adults in the lives of infants are ultimately superordinate because the survival of infants depends upon them, it is also true that by the end of the phase of infancy, some infants have been known to achieve the upper hand in important social terms.

It is apparent that the social situation that includes infants and adults is very far from simple. It is further complicated by the fact that adults usually feel personally related to their infants and it is a relationship that is freighted with expectations, notions of responsibility, preconceived ideas of a shared future, fantasies of the infant's achievements in all its future transformations. At the same time, for infants the associations are better described as dependence than relationship, insofar as the latter implies personal reciprocities. It is true that infants are often sources of great satisfaction to their mothering ones, and dissatisfactions, but their nature is unknown to infants and is a by-product of associations and cultural experience that has nothing to do with particular infants. For infants, attendants are sources of satisfaction and security, or not, not individuated persons with needs and satisfactions of their own. Besides, they would be unable to provide for these adults even if they could identify their needs.

The illusion of personal significance is often maintained for mothering ones by the essentially magical manipulation of adults by infants and young children. Their pre-conceptual level of mental development makes it impossible for them to recognize the connections between events and people other than their immediate juxtaposition in particular time and place, or to understand the sequence of activities that leads from their indication of need to its satisfaction. But they learn very quickly to present the sounds and gestures that facilitate the appearance of satisfaction, including the comfort that flows to them from the satisfaction they evoke in their mothering ones. After all, it does not take long for a puppy to "sit up and beg" once this has been revealed to be an irresistible cue for being fed. Excessive collaboration by adults in this kind of magical exchange can seriously interfere with progress in the social development of the young.

It is not difficult to observe adults who manage to live with the few interpersonal skills they acquired in infancy and with little more. They have added some cultural elaborations, but their social competence has not proceeded much further. There are adults who have made extreme dependency a way of life. It is, after all, highly coercive. Hypochondria, helplessness, flattery, are useful to this end. The "little woman" bit in relation to males often works. It may become increasingly difficult to find mothering ones as time goes on, but some people manage. Even when they do not, more competent people often take over simply to get something done. This is a narrow and restricted way of life for an adult, but it is possible and, for some, satisfying. At least, nothing else has apparently seemed more attractive. For others, by the time they become aware of alternatives, they have become too personally handicapped to pursue them. The magical use of the cry is perhaps even more common among adults to which the magical use of words is added. The effective tear or sob is not abandoned by a great many, magical words (to be discussed shortly) even less so. Finally, the chief coercions of infancy, manipulation of access to satisfactions and increase and decrease in tenderness, remain basic coercions for all adults, however elaborate their cultural disguises. Thus, much that is socially useful is even acquired in infancy.

However, extensive use of infantile devices by adults suggests that some serious interference with further development has occurred because infantile resources are limited and crude and all human beings except the seriously defective harbor potentialities for more effective means to survival and satisfactions. The biological impulses to realize biological potentialities are strong.

Biological growth is a continuing factor of great importance. If it does not proceed normally, social development will be impeded. When it does, new resources become available for cultivation. For social development, the most significant new biological resource available at the end of infancy is the growing capacity for distinguishing and producing sounds and patterning them. Sound-making is important from birth, as we have seen. It is the chief tool for influencing others. The characteristic cry of newborn infants becomes differentiated rather quickly. In time, infants reach what is called "the babbling phase." Cries break up into sounds. Once the ability for this is available, and it is apparently associated with refinements of hearing and sound production that are outcomes of growth, sound differentiation and patterning is developed by emulation of what is heard and by the deliberate efforts of adults to encourage some patterns and repress others. People wheeling baby buggies can be heard saying over and over again: "Mama," "Dada," Doggie, doggie." "No, not Gaga—Mama," and so on and on. This seems silly to passersby, but it is a vital service to infants. Finally, infants begin to play with sounds, to practice their production. Then one day they succeed in producing "mama" or "dada." The response of mothering ones is tremendous. Their relation to their infants changes entirely when they come to regard them as capable of using language, and with it, they erroneously assume, thought. In fact, this initial performance by infants merely indicates that capacities for these activities are beginning to be available. The use of the first vocabulary is as magical as the use of the cry. All that infants know is that it works.

These additions, associated with physical growth and changes induced in mothering ones, marks the transition from infancy to childhood. The appearance of capacity for speech is its threshold.

Chapter Three

Childhood

THE MOVE from one stage of social development to another is neither abrupt nor complete. New resources and abilities are added, but they do not necessarily or always replace those that preceded them. There is a tendency in the initial phases of a stage of development to use new resources in old ways. For example, children use their first words as magically as they have used their cries. In adult life, people operate on different levels of development depending on the area of activity and the kind of people involved. The most highly evolved individuals are likely to behave in a childish, or juvenile, or adolescent fashion with some people and in some social situations. What distinguishes a new phase of development is the fact that an individual manifests some capacities and traits that he could not before. What determines the social classification of particular individuals is the level of social skill that characterizes most of their routine encounters with people.

Furthermore, stages of development are cumulative. Most of the resources and relationships and cultural traits and social abilities of all levels, once established, continue to be important assets for life. Those of early phases are simply insufficient for meeting the individual and collective demands of later ones, not necessarily useless. Indeed, the appearance of abilities, such as ability for conceptual thought or for the precise use of language, or for competition and voluntary cooperation, depend on the development of the resources of infancy and childhood. If this is not accomplished during these periods of physical growth they must be cultivated in later life before abilities, potentially available to physically adult humans, can be manifest by them. In essence, this is the basic problem in the re-habilitation of adolescents and youths who have been socially retarded or who dropped out somewhere along the way. It is more difficult to supply the necessary relation-ships and social situations that characterize actual stages of physical growth once individuals are beyond them. Physical maturity and the resources that go with it modify the pos-sibilities for the application of the coercions required to evoke cultural modifications of organic systems and func-tions and lead to the acquisition of important additions to the cultural repertoires of individuals.

Each stage of development is best construed as an addi-tion of a new cluster of relevant factors to a continuous series of events rather than as something discrete and self-contained.

The psychobiological resources that become available with the physical growth characteristic of childhood that are of special relevance for social development are the capacity for speech and the beginning capacity for using it as true language, the beginning of conceptualization, and a very great increase in physiological stability and physical coordination.

Motor skills, manual dexterity, and precise perception are vital supports for social development. One of the problems in the social development of physically handicapped chil-dren is that their handicap keeps them socially dependent and so interferes with their progress toward social autonomy. The physical resources of children make for a degree of organic antonomy that is far superior to that of infants and it is this that markedly decreases dependence on others. Children cannot survive on their own, but they acquire enough coordination and mobility to introduce new forms-of-interaction with their elders. Their increased powers of perception and conception speed up the differen-tiation of their experience. As a result, "mothering ones," who are apparently perceived as vague sources of satisfac-tion only crudely distinguished as separate entities by in-fants, are identified as different people and connected with specific satisfactions and dissatisfactions by children.

All of this is greatly augmented by the child's new and growing ability to organize his experience by the use of symbols associated with meanings, coupled with his ability for speech and language performance. Children, with few exceptions, are not capable of abstract thought or of attaching validated meaning to words that stand for abstractions or non-sensible qualities, such as truth and beauty. But they do develop conceptions of spatial relationships, of sequence, of the separateness of their organisms from things, people and events, and of some connections between these that are independent of themselves. Children can effectively conceptualize what can be verified by their senses. The words that come to have precise and consensually valid meanings for them are those that refer to physical objects and persons and visible action. Concrete nouns and active verbs are the first to be transformed from magical words into effective words for communicating specific things to others and receiving specific communications from them.

The first conceptually organized experience centers around the visible and concrete. Adults point to chairs, tables, baby, mother, dogs running, and speak the words that refer to them in the language their children are expected to acquire. After considerable repetition, a child begins to associate chair with the particular one indicated. At first he cannot grasp the possibilities for generalization that a word provides. He does not immediately identify a very different kind of chair, upholstered rather than his little red wooden chair, for example, as a chair. But with the assistance of adults who point to all kinds of chairs, using the same word as they do so, and with his expanding psychobiological capacity, the child soon acquires a true concept, in this instance, "chair." Because it can stand for all chairs of all kinds that have existed, do exist, and will exist, anywhere, the whole realm of "chairness," so to speak, is separated from undifferentiated experience and separated from "tableness" and "mothering" and "doggieness," ad infinitum, as well.

The fact that chairs of a great variety of physical characteristics, of different uses, present to the senses and not, can all be subsumed under the concept and word "chair" is an instance of the extraordinary potentialities of human mental resources. It is this ability that separates mankind from all other animals. It is this that makes it possible for human beings to create the social realm, and live in large numbers complexly organized, and escape, in some measure, constant preoccupation with immediate experience and the pursuit of each day's food, clothing, and shelter. This conceptual grasp of experience and the universe, complexly and still mysteriously related to the central nervous system and sense organs, is necessary for human consciousness and human memory and human powers of recall. It requires words associated with consensually validated meanings to function and it is apparently words that hold the items conceived in memory that makes communicable recall possible.

The beginning of the development of this extraordinary human ability occurs in childhood. This is what most sharply separates childhood from infancy. But the capacities of children in this regard are limited. They fall far short of what is required for competent adult life. The characteristic mode of conceptualization in childhood has been called "parataxic" by Harry Stack Sullivan[1] and "autistic" by Jean Piaget.[2] Sullivan uses the word "autistic" to refer to the typical use of words by children. These men refer to the same phenomenon, namely, that aside from concepts and words related to what is apparent to the senses, the conceptions of children of what goes on around them are highly individual. They do not grasp at all the consensually validated referents and meanings that adults have in mind when they use abstract terms and refer to non-material phenomena. They do not immediately grasp the characterizing qualities of meanings that seem self-evident to cultivated adults even when they refer to concrete phenomena. However, children *can* acquire precise concepts of these and they *can* associate a vocabulary of words that refer to what they perceive with validated meanings. This ability is what Piaget calls "conceptual realism."

None of this develops unless attendant adults make an

---

[1] Sullivan, *op. cit., Conceptions.*

[2] Jean Piaget, *The Language and Thought of the Child* (New York: World Publishing Company, 1955); and *Six Psychological Studies* (New York: Random House, 1967).

effort to use the abilities of children for conceptualization and linguistic performance and train them for both. Their attention must be directed and a language must be provided. All infants, except defective ones, are born with the potential for uttering the range of sounds that fall within human capacity. But languages are built of particular combinations of sound and the patterning of sound-making begins in infancy and is greatly advanced in childhood. Some of it is picked up by emulation, but a great deal of it depends upon deliberate effort by adults to evoke imitation, and their correction of error. This is so effective that by the time most people have reached physical adulthood they cannot pronounce or hear some combinations of sound that are not incorporated in their own language. Some accent that results from the intrusion of the sound patterns that belong to their original language is discernible in the speech of most people who use a language learned after childhood. Some new sound patterns are forever missing.

The acquisition of the rudiments of language is probably the most important cultural accomplishment of childhood. It is not only the sound patterns and the substantial vocabulary that are acquired, but syntax and rhythm and expressive connotations are also picked up by children almost entirely without deliberate effort on their part and little on the part of the adults around them. This does not constitute knowledge of the language, in the sense of conscious conceptual formulations of its characteristics. Many adults are ignorant of the grammar of the languages they speak well. This is an integrated addition to the psychobiological apparatus for linguistic and mental activity. Vocabulary outstrips the acquisition of collective meaning for children and, therefore, much of the language of children remains highly individual in meaning and magical in use, autistic, in short. This is the source of a great deal of future confusion because adults tend to assume that words have specific referents. They often fail to identify the autistic survivals that are to be found in the linguistic performances of everyone. How much of this is eliminated for each individual after childhood depends upon the extent to which his early vocabulary has been subjected to deliberate attention.

In literate societies, competent linguistic performance depends upon the acquisition of a written as well as an oral language. For most adults, the two are experienced as one, although some of them do notice that they speak better and more easily than they write, or vice versa, and some do not find reading anything more than their daily paper easy or rewarding. Clearly, oral and written languages are not the same. The acquisition of one does not automatically provide a grasp of the other.[3] Written language depends much more on conceptual skills than oral language does; in fact, written language is doubly abstract because it represents oral language. Obviously, it does not involve the elaborate apparatus for speech, but it does require complex perceptual abilities and manual dexterity and their coordination. The fact that adults have so fused their oral and written languages that they conceive of them as mere extensions of each other, or manifestations of the same thing in different form, is a glaring example of selective inattention and the quite marvelous way in which very complicated and imposed modifications of human organisms become unified and automatic processes by repetition.

Obviously, infants have no resources that can be used by their elders to start their preparation for written communication, as sound-patterning prepares them for speech. Moreover, children are not psychobiologically equipped for mastering a written language. They have neither the conceptual skills nor the manual dexterity. But training for this can begin in childhood and does in literate societies. What is cultivated for the purpose is the increased perceptual range and precision of children and beginning conceptual capacity.

Their training starts with the identification of pictures of things. Adults are so used to the almost instant association of a picture with the object represented that it does not occur to most of them that this is a very complicated process indeed, and not well understood either. There is no very clear identity between a live, tawny, Persian cat, that

---

[3] For brief discussion refer to "Linguistics: A Modern View of Language," by Henry Lee Smith, Jr. in *Man's Knowledge of the World* ed. by Lyman Bryson (New York: McGraw-Hill, 1960), p. 342. This volume has other excellent articles on the organic factors that are relevant.

is perhaps a child's pet, and a black and white photograph of a Siamese kitten, or even a photograph of his own cat for that matter. That human beings come to make connections between such empirically different objects is an example of the truly marvelous potentialities of human mental equipment.

Children who are provided with the means develop the ability to make hundreds of such associations and to make fine discriminations between representations as well. For example, they not only separate pictures of cats from dogs, from tables, from people, etc., but they can even come to recognize that pictures of their pets as young animals represent those pets full grown. Further, they become able to associate oral words with the pictures as well as the live object. And those who are presented with the printed words appropriate to the pictures are able to connect them with the appropriate oral words, pictures, and live pets. Some children can read simple sentences by the end of childhood.

This is an immensely complex social achievement. It depends upon the presence of adults who can provide the pictures and letters and printed words and who are ready and willing to present them in conjunction to their children over and over again. This not only uses the resources of the children that are immediately available; it encourages their growth and development. In literate societies, this cultivation is a giant step in a long series of developments that are essential for adult competence in them. Any child in such societies who is not so cultivated is socially handicapped.

A substantial repertoire of manners, folkways, and mores is also transmitted to children in the same ways that language and concepts are, namely, by their elders' exhortations and repetitive demonstrations and the children's imitation and rote-learning. Since little of this is ever subjected to logical thought, and it is intergrated as part of the psychobiological processes themselves, once acquired, this cultural addition is experienced as "natural." How natural is demonstrated by the fact that individuals tend to respond to their use of their own language as though it were part of their biological equipment, like moving their arms and legs or hearing and seeing. In a real sense, it is.

This determination of the functioning of the physical apparatus for speech is a conspicuous example of the cultural modification of organic structure and function. It is clear that there is nothing superficial about it. What is true for auditory and laryngeal structures is true for others in some measure. Breathing, posture, gait, digestion, elimination, perception, and so forth, are all patterned in some ways according to cultural impositions by the people who raise the young. Most important of all, perhaps, the store of conceptual formulations that are the conspicuous feature of human minds and that are necessary for complex mental activity depend upon the cultural resources made available to them. Since cultural items can only be provided by people already imbued with them, cultural transmission is social transmission. The careless use of the word culture with active verbs distorts reality. Culture does not do anything or compel anyone. Particular other people coerce each individual to acquire a particular cultural repertoire. Cultural phenomena neither create, maintain, transmit, nor impose themselves.

The transmission of culture to children is as vital a necessity for their survival and achievement of maturity as feeding them. Their new capacities for conceptual and linguistic activity greatly expand the range of what their elders can do for them in this respect and fortunate children are so tended that by the end of childhood they acquire considerable ability to identify a large range of things and people and to anticipate what they can and cannot do.

It is precisely the lack of this kind of attention and cultural training that results in the difficulties of learning in school that characterize children from culturally and personally deprived homes. The "Head Start" program recently introduced to prepare some of them for formal education is designed to supply it. There is no reason why it cannot be done deliberately by people who are strangers to the children, but it is more difficult to achieve and probably takes longer than when it is done routinely in families and started in infancy. Whether or not it can be extensively developed in adolescents if it has not been substantially started earlier is questionable. Childhood is the period in which it is most effectively initiated.

The interpersonal relationships, cultural additions, forms of coercion and forms of interaction that characterize childhood are largely the consequences of both the needs that these important new resources of children evoke and the abilities they engender.

It is their new conceptual capacity that greatly augments the ability of children to differentiate experience that makes them aware of the multiple and heterogeneous relationships that actually constitute the family settings, or substitutes for them, in which they have existed from their beginning, but which, from their point of view as infants, was experienced as an encompassing environment that included vague presences to which they responded with very crude discriminations. As they move into the social phase of childhood, children clearly perceive that they have two parents, and siblings if any, and become aware of a "home circle" that includes more distant relatives, family friends and acquaintances, servants and servicing people, as well as the family members who are residents of the household. They become aware that this household population constitutes a stable network of relationships that is independent of their connections with each one of them. In short, it is in childhood that human beings first become aware of a group as distinct from a paired relationship.

This discovery is made in the home by most children when they notice that other people are among the factors that deflect the attention of ministering adults away from them and interfere with their access to satisfactions. The initial response to this discovery is usually an attempt to eliminate the interference, either by doing something that requires attention, often by the use of the cry and the non-cooperation that worked in their infancy, or by trying to move the other out of the way. If these maneuvers do not work, and in most cases they do not, children have no recourse but adaptation to the situation.

How well children adapt to this first awareness of group organization, something that transcends the reciprocities between any two people in it and imposes some restraints on all participants, has great importance for their future development. Until children discover that group organization is itself a source of satisfactions that paired relationships cannot supply and, especially, of security, and that it does not always prevent access to particular other people in paired relationships, they experience the group as a threat to their welfare and will try to break it up insofar as it impinges directly upon them.

Since participation in groups is increasingly the means to satisfaction and security for individuals, the ability to live in them comfortably and willingness to contribute to their maintenance is essential to adult social competence and individual welfare. This *can* be learned in childhood and it is an important responsibility of people who rear the young to see that it is. Initially, this requires the same coercions employed in the cultivation of other social and cultural skills. The parent, or other training elders, who, by continued indulgence of dependence and egocentric demands in children, interferes with their adaptation to group living, does them a great disservice. Incompetence for participation in groups all but precludes the negotiation of the next stage of social development, the juvenile, and becomes an increasing handicap as time goes on.

This is the sociological situation that has been called the "Oedipal phase" by psychiatrists and psychologists since Freud first so clearly described the difficulties that children manifest at this stage of development and some of the consequences of failure to resolve them that can be observed in adults. In my opinion, the "Oedipal" explanation is fanciful, overelaborate, and makes the explanation of these manifestations in females impossibly complex. Besides, the Freudian overemphasis on the family unit as the sole determinant of personal development clouds the fact that children react to anyone whom they notice interfering with their access to a person who provides their satisfactions, not merely to their male parents. If fathers are important "mothering ones," the appearance of the actual mother at a time when the child expects his father's full attention produces the same effects as those that Freudians assume apply only to mothers. As Malinowsky pointed out, among the Trobriand Islanders maternal uncles evoke the kind of behavior that fathers do most often among West Europeans since it is the Trobriand uncles who perform the social functions that fathers do among Europeans.

Whether or not the Freudian libidinal explanation of the behavior is deemed correct, the need in childhood for new social skills that further curtail egocentric impulses produces strains that evoke similar behavior in children everywhere until their adaptation to their newly perceived social situation, a group, is achieved. It is also true that for most children, but not all, this development is initiated in family groups. Participation in groups does not merely curtail individual impulses, it interferes with pairing as well, and children have come to recognize their direct relationships with others and to make some important distinctions between them. Therefore, they resist interference with them as well as further limitations on their own impulses.

Because children begin to recognize that adults are their source of the means to their satisfactions, they begin to view them with considerable respect. Adults are a source of satisfaction and security and of anxiety in almost equal proportions for children. They have much less impact on each other. Their egocentricity and their degree of helplessness make children of little use to one another except as assistants in play and sources of stimulation to action, verbal and mental as well as physical. Children pay attention to juveniles or pre-adolescents or adolescents, indeed to anyone who is older than they are who can regulate them and their environment. With one another they remain essentially absorbed in their own states. Even when they talk to one another and play together they do not listen and do not expect consistent answers and responses. They indulge in what Piaget calls "collective monologue."[4] Children have no capacities for dealing with peers.

Limited though it is, the significant interpersonal sphere of childhood is much larger and more complex than that of infancy. Parents, siblings, and all the others who regularly impinge on children, once they are experienced as separate entities, are simultaneously experienced as different sources of satisfactions and dissatisfactions. They also present a variety of personal and cultural traits to which children respond in different ways. They begin to recognize people as persons, in some measure. In short, children, in contrast

[4] Compare Piaget, *op. cit.*, p. 49; *Language and Thought*, p. 75.

to infants, begin to have relationships, not merely dependencies.

Relationship *per se* is difficult to describe and has not been explained. We do not establish relationships with everyone who provides for us and we do establish relationships with many who provide little other than their presence. But whatever a relationship is, it seems to involve an actual exchange of energy, or an investment of energy into the person or object or activity to which we become related. Relationships are manifest in action also. Apparently, the energy involved is transformed into a felt need to act with respect to, or on behalf of, the object to which we are related. This is, I suppose, what is meant by the word "commitment." When a complaint is made that a person is not committed it does not imply that he is not present, or does not use the resources provided by a person or social situation, or even that he does not in some measure act with respect to them. It does imply that he has not invested his own energies into these objects to any marked degree, that he will take from them but will give to them only what he is coerced to give. He has not made a store of energy available for use by others or for the maintenance of something independent of his immediate impulses.

A relationship to a particular other person involves something of this nature. The participants become aware of a sensible connection with one another, not tangible but full of meaning. Relationships are described as "ties" or "bonds." Their meanings are various and change with respect to the same object, but in all cases someone or something or some activity has significance that is distinct from the significance of one's own organism or one's own personal attributes. The significance may be highly instrumental, but the object is at least recognized as an important instrument. Although I do not fully subscribe to the Freudian definition of "libido," I think that Freud's conception of "libidinal investment," insofar as it describes an energy transformation and investment, is in accord with the facts of life.

When two people have established such an energy exchange with each other, whatever evokes it and however it comes about, the intrusion of a third element, person, thing, event, into the exchange between them has very real impact. The more involved the relationship the greater the impact. To the extent that a third element draws the attention and energy of one participant to itself, it deflects them from another. As Georg Simmel pointed out, the addition of one to two does not augment the two, it breaks up their pairing, however temporarily. If the pairing provides exceptional satisfactions, the intrusion is felt as a major blow. If it is unsatisfactory and evokes anxiety, an intrusion may be experienced as a rescue and relief. In any case, there is a drastic shift in the states of the participants.

It is obvious to most adults that twosomes are not adequate for all purposes and that groups and larger organizations can provide security and satisfaction that pairs cannot. But children have only newly discovered paired relationships and when, hard upon that discovery, they note that these are frequently subject to the influences of a larger social configuration which often dilutes the effects of pairings, or brings them to an end, their first impulses are to maintain the pairings. Adaptation to groups involves a diffusion of energies by their members. It takes experience to discover that advantages accrue from the group situation and to become able to regulate the energies that are involved in relationships so that they operate effectively in more than one type of social configuration.

The achievement of this social competence is a most important step in the social development of children. It does not immediately prepare them to participate in larger social organizations, but it is a vital preparation for so doing. It does not move them far out of the limits of their egocentricity, but it expands those limits. Children not only develop capacity for some reciprocity with individuals in paired association, limited though it be, but they begin to be able to cooperate voluntarily as units in group contexts. Children are not intellectually capable of "putting themselves in the place of others" and so they do not experience the intrinsic value of others, but they do become aware of others as important sources of their own satisfactions and development and security—not that they could so conceive this—and insofar as they are, others are viewed by children as important and with respect. Since other children are *not* usually sources of what they need and want, the relationships of most children are to adults or older young people, not to each other. Because some others are recognized as important, children are amenable to compromise and voluntarily offer a great deal of cooperation to adults, though not to each other.

None of this extremely important social development in children can occur unless adults use their powers of coercion to achieve it. They have a number of potent means for so doing at their command. Control of access to essential satisfactions by adults remains a powerful coercion on children. So does increase and decrease of tenderness displayed toward their young. But important new coercions are added as a result of the capacity of children to speak and conceptualize. Once this ability appears, adults assume that the young have a "mind" and are, therefore, ready for serious training. They begin to verbalize clearly formulated approvals and disapprovals and to reinforce these with systematic rewards and punishments. Childhood is conspicuously a period of "do's" and "don't's."

If these coercions were merely verbal and active they would go far toward evoking in children the restraints on and elaborations of their responses desired by their elders. Those that became habit and automatic would be stable and hard to change. Resistance to change would lie chiefly in the absence of attention involved in automatic behavior. Demand for change would not be likely to evoke passionate defense for the status quo. This is true for many adaptations to technical changes. Drivers of cars with nonautomatic gears may reach for them for some time after they acquire a car with an automatic shift, but few hold out against the change and insist on the older arrangement. Certainly they do not make a "moral" issue of it. People who move into new quarters reach for their toothbrushes on the "old side," confuse the water taps, turn on the wrong burners on their stoves, head in the wrong direction for their front doors, for some time, but they do not resist adaptation to their new environment. Habits persist, but not all of them are experienced as immutable in principle.

There are some that are, however, and many of these are acquired even in childhood. Would an electric candle be substituted for a wax one on a church altar, for example? Could pressing a light switch have the same moral effect as lighting a taper? Is frozen food really healthy for people who grew up in kitchens where women prepared their own? Isn't there something reprehensible that requires elaborate justification about sleeping till almost noon for those whose parents thought it was? And if the suggestion of change in these small acts evokes feelings of diminished personal worth and apprehension of vague disaster, demand for changes in notions of propriety in relations to others, especially to people in authority, and to supernatural beings, or of the social and cultural aspects of eating and drinking and sexual behavior and body-functions, are likely to evoke awesome intimations of imminent catastrophe. "What is the world coming to?" is a frequent comment of the older generation on changes of this kind, and they imply that it must be coming to a bad end.

The reason for this is that the verbal admonitions and direct punishments of children by elders is accompanied by the evocation of anxiety in them. Some of this is unintentional, but it is inevitable because the expression of disapproval or threat of it by elders suggests rejection of themselves to the young—even abandonment—and their degree of dependence makes these dire threats. This plight of children is often used deliberately. Parents and others add threats of "bogey men" who will take naughty children away, of putting them out of the home, of powers that will make their hands drop off if they touch what is forbidden, etc., to their commands and prohibitions.

Anxiety is far more uncomfortable than the pain of a spanking or deprivation of dessert or the opportunity to participate in a particular activity, because it is vague and pervasive. Most of these anxiety-provoking statements cannot be put to an empirical test. Even such remarks as "Mother won't love you if——," or "You are bad and wicked and will come to a bad end" suggest both unspecified and future disaster. They put children in the position of waiting, which is uncomfortable in itself, and of waiting for something unknown and unpleasant besides, which is worse. Everywhere children are raised on an "anxiety gradient," as Harry Stack Sullivan called it, a graduated series of threats of unknown consequences linked with the host of things they are told they should and should not do and situations that they may or may not enter into. When children do what their elders wish them to do no anxiety follows. On the contrary, their compliance is usually associated with the achievement of some specific satisfactions. The satisfaction responses of their elders tend to augment the satisfactions of the young. But when children misbehave, from the point of view of their elders, they not only are deprived of satisfactions, but are threatened with withdrawal of the attentions of their supporters and are promised the highly undesirable attentions of unseen powers besides.

Infants can be made anxious, usually by the transmission of the anxiety of their mothering ones via the paths of empathy. However, most infants escape the direct evocation of much anxiety because this is a response to negative elements in an interpersonal situation and, strictly speaking, infants have no personal relationships. These begin to be differentiated only in childhood and this differentiation is accompanied by the evocation of anxiety as the indicator of whether or not children are in good standing with those on whom they rely for maintenance and cultivation. It is in childhood that anxiety and its derivatives—embarrassment, shame, anger, etc.—begin to serve as indicators of social disapproval and dissatisfaction for everyone.

Because anxiety in all its forms is so uncomfortable, and because everyone needs the cooperation of some others, individuals take on some of the social and cultural requirements of their training elders as personal traits both to guarantee access to their help and to avoid anxiety. The traits that have been imposed along with large doses of anxiety people come to feel must be defended at all cost for the rest of life. Anxiety, or the threat of it, not only ensures the continuation of some things, it ensures the avoidance of much that is new and/or significantly different. Because the absence of anxiety is associated with positive indications of approval for particular traits and performance, not merely the absence of disapproval, social security begins to depend on assurance that whatever a person is or does has been tested and found acceptable. Thus, the merely unknown or strange becomes a source of anxiety and "what other people think" is a vital concern throughout the lives of most people. This anxiety-enforcement of social and cultural demands made by elders on the young is the basis not only of their own personal stability, but of the tenacity with which generations of people perpetuate their organizations and institutions. Whether or not this is an asset depends upon the degree of physical, economic, social, and cultural change that characterizes particular times and places.

The new psychobiological resources of children and the conspicuous additions to their interpersonal exchanges result in new forms-of-interaction between children and the people around them. Superordination and subordination are not the only modes of relationship open to them. They develop considerable ability for compromise and cooperation. The submission of infants to adult manipulation cannot rightly be called either. As children begin to notice some of the intervening factors between their desires and their satisfactions and to identify and differentiate between their "mothering ones," they also begin to recognize that there are limits to their own powers. Their world becomes less magical. They begin to see that in order to get and keep something desirable they have to give up something, either in the form of an inhibition of some other impulse, or the sharing of the source of satisfaction with others, or even, in some instances, the repression of some impulses altogether. They also discover that the people who begin noticeably to populate their world can be useful in the pursuit of their own satisfactions and security and that the aid of some others is necessary. Compromise and cooperation follow from this recognition.

This does not imply that other people are experienced as more than instrumental means to egocentric ends. Children remain utterly egocentric. Their self-regulation depends upon their recognition of their own inability to achieve what they desire singlehanded. They do not act out of consideration for others or because they "take the place of others" and so, presumably, act with respect to their condition, as suggested by George Mead. Children do not have the conceptual ability to infer the states and conditions of other people. The best they can do is note their impact on their own. And so, children compromise and cooperate with others only when the possibility of satisfaction is clearly in sight or when they are aware that non-compliance will lead to unpleasant consequences. They do not voluntarily limit their impulses or direct their behavior in the ways that their elders want them to on behalf of vague and long-term goals, or to satisfy the needs of others, or because they love them. They are quite incapable of loving anyone, even themselves.

These are the psychobiological and social and cultural ingredients that are particularly useful for the social development of children. They are more numerous, varied, and complex by far than those of infancy. The utilization of these resources by adults not only begins to prepare children to live among people in general, but goes far toward making them identifiable members of particular families and societies. The language and the repertoire of symbols and meanings that children acquire as part of their apparatus for linguistic and mental activities are only partly useful for living with all other human beings. Only the ability to use a language for communication and mental operations in general are universal. The cultural content required for both is overwhelmingly local.

By the end of childhood, children everywhere are very perceptibly the children of a particular society and of parts thereof. Their ability to live in another requires the modification or suppression of some of their cultural acquisitions as well as additions to their cultural repertoires. This is clearly apparent in the language performance of children. Their "mother tongue" already seems like part of their organic equipment to them. They are even beginning to lose some of their initial ability to pattern sounds other than those used in their own language. If they move to live among people who speak a different language, their own is not much help. Accents are sometimes ineradicable, which indicates that some sound patterning can no longer be changed and some other sound patterns can no longer be acquired. What is true of language is equally true of many other cultural modifications established in childhood. The mark of social relationships remains.

Thus, some of the limitations of childhood persist into the adult life of everyone. Parataxic mental constructs and the autistic use of many words are to be found in the performances of any adult. So is the magical use of words. The fact that people acquire vocabulary and symbols far in advance of even the ability to acquire consensually validated meanings and referents for them, leaves everyone with a heritage of mental and linguistic equipment of dubious utility. Some of it works fairly well as long as they live with people raised in the same social and cultural settings. For example, "I'm sorry" and "I love you" are magical phrases that generations of children in the United States have discovered will deflect the most panic-making threats by parents and other caretakers. They continue to serve the same purpose for thousands of adults even though they insulate individuals from the likelihood of improvements of destructive and ineffective performances and their relations with spouses, colleagues, and others, continue on their unsatisfactory course. Shared magic is quite effective in any language. But it is a serious impediment to communication and effective cooperation between people with different word magic, and it interferes with rational processes and arrangements. This does not apply to individuals alone. The effects of local enculturation are cumulative and influence the exchanges between populations as such. The use of similar vocabularies with different meanings by international servants is a major impediment to international cooperation.

Both as a result of the accidents of life and of particular cultural selection, some proportion of adult populations fails to develop far beyond the social capacities of childhood. This is not infrequently prescribed for women and subjugated people. It follows that for these people the coercions and social configurations that characterize childhood as a stage of development are the ones that are important for them as adults. Family units are overwhelmingly the most important for women and subordinate populations, and are the units in which they live most of their lives. Furthermore, adult children, as well as chronological ones, lack sufficient conceptual grasp of the material and social realms in which they live, and even of their own experience, to live comfortably without supervision by authorities. They need, and often demand, hierarchical order and authoritarian leadership. Childish adults are by no means absent even in the most sophisticated populations and important social consequences stem from this fact.

The adults who "escape from freedom," to use Erich Fromm's[5] phrase, who are the most enthusiastic followers of authoritarian leaders, who are most likely to accept authoritarian dogmas and rituals without question, who are domineering when they can be and subservient when they cannot, are people whose social abilities remain essentially those of childhood. They are often skillful, except in areas that require tact in human relationships or competence in abstract thought. They tend to oversimplify when they evaluate social situations, or any other. Their differentiations are based on crude indices and are, therefore, insufficiently defined. These people tend to experience people and situations as clearly one thing or another, rather than as items on a continuum most of which lie between its extremes. Yet, despite the assurance with which these people declare something to be "this or that" at a given time, they are likely to declare it to be "that or this" soon after if their particular authorities change their policies.

Clearly, adult life can be lived agreeably enough with the resources of childhood, if these have been well developed, as long as the overall social context provides authority and directives that protect socially childish adults from complex social relationships and the need to cope with abstract and general concepts. The mastery of living in groups in which authority is clearly indicated gives them scope enough for family life, religious practice, occupations, and political participation. The scope is narrower than it need be and it makes these people vulnerable in the face of drastic changes in the conditions in which they live, unless they have a leader to follow; but in stable circumstances, socially childish adults do not fare badly. However, human beings have more social potential than this stage of development encompasses and, except in those social situations for

[5] Erich Fromm, *Escape from Freedom* (New York: Farrar & Rinehart, 1941).

which cultural norms prescribe the social developments of childhood as the ones that are appropriate for adult relationships and activities, most human beings are more elaborately cultivated and move on to more complex levels of social life.

If the potentialities of childhood are realized, enough autonomy is achieved to make it possible for children to maintain fairly stable relations and to cooperate with other children for substantial periods of time without the presence of their elders. Children begin to discover that for some purposes children like themselves are more useful than their elders. They begin to seek them out and to avoid adult supervision. This development marks the threshold of a new stage of development. The children are becoming juveniles.

Chapter Four

Juvenile

THE JUVENILE STAGE of social development is separated from childhood by a level of cultivation of psychobiological resources that changes the social context in which the young live rather than by the addition of psychobiological elements that are conspicuously new. Growth, in this period of somatic development, is chiefly the expansion of existing resources and greater stability and coordination. But consequences of great importance for social development follow from the psychobiological potentialities of juveniles, chiefly because they enable them to establish stable associations with their peers for the first time.

The need for peers and the development of ability to form comfortable relationships with them are the outstanding characteristics of the juvenile phase of social development. Since adult life is so largely made up of peer associations, the successful negotiation of this stage is of vital significance to individuals and to the effective maintenance and functions of collective arrangements. The juvenile era is preeminently one that establishes individual capacity for membership in multiple peer organizations.

Increase in the physiological stability of juveniles, especially in their capacity for muscular coordination and their coordination of perception and manual dexterity, releases them from the extreme dependency on elders and their continuous intervention into their on-going activities that characterizes childhood. It is possible for juveniles to spend considerable time together outside of the range of the supervision of adults without danger to themselves.

Increased mental capacity, especially the beginning of conceptual operations, and the acquisition of considerable precision in the use of language, greatly expand the grasp by juveniles of the nature of the world around them. The ordering of their experience by the use of symbols and meanings is conspicuously augmented. Memory has become a useful repository of experience open to orderly and relevant recall. The physical realm can be extensively explored. The realm of relationships begins to be reliably differentiated though not greatly understood. The nature of adult relationships is beyond juvenile understanding. Relationships between individual juveniles are relatively superficial. The great importance of groups to juveniles curbs their egocentric impulses, but does not dispel their egocentricity. The needs of others as individuals are not usually compelling to juveniles.

The conceptual capacity of juveniles should not be overrated. Their ability to expand their experience by the use of symbols and concepts detached from direct experience remains extremely limited. Consensually validated meaning for words and experiences is still largely limited for juveniles to what can be verified by their senses and communicated to one another. Much of their thought remains highly individuated (parataxic) and their use of many words is still autistic. However, the action-oriented exchanges between juveniles and their intolerance of one another serve to refine both their language performance and their formulations of their experience. They are used to what is nonsense from their viewpoint emanating from adults, but they do not put up with it from one another. Therefore, the peer associations of juveniles take each of them a long way toward the establishment of a dependable repertoire of symbols and meanings and a precise use of words. So does direct tutoring by and apprenticeship to elders. In the course of their transmission of skills and information to juveniles, in contrast to their ethical exhortations, adults tend to be concrete and precise also. They view juveniles as ready for formal education and training and devote themselves to their cultivation in rather specific things. The juvenile period is essentially a "how to do it" era. It is active and realistic.

Chronological juveniles remain dependent on adults for maintenance, protection, and training, but their new capacity for dependable associations with one another changes their experience of authority. It takes them beyond their home circles into schools, churches, other homes, and thereby confronts them with variety in the demands and judgments of elders and authorities. Juveniles can become aware that authority need not be monolithic. This discovery can be disturbing to juveniles initially, but the new support available to them of their peer-groups tends to allay anxieties that may be aroused in individual juveniles by the discovery that their particular elders are not omniscient and omnipotent and turn the new experience into an opportunity to exercise choice. It is an expansion of social freedom.

This is enhanced by the nature of juvenile peer-groups which introduce an altogether new kind of authority, namely, the *prima inter pares*, first among equals. Authority in families and schools, etc., is inevitably a dominance to which the young can only submit or rebel. But leadership in juvenile peer-groups is chosen by the membership and it is maintained by its consent. It can be unseated in the same way. Compliance to this kind of authority is experienced as deference rather than submission. This experience is enhanced by the fact that many decisions in these peer-groups are made as a result of discussion between all members. This new degree of control over individual fate is one of the important reasons why membership in these groups is so exhilarating to juveniles.

The first effective experience of relationships with equals is the peer-group participation of juveniles. They do not have the capacity for maintaining stable paired associations with one another that are not oriented to membership in these groups. Contrary to their own convictions about their experience, and of widespread evaluations of juvenile relationships by adults, juveniles do not view one another as intrinsically valuable or important. It is their peer-groups that have intrinsic significance, not their peers. That this is so, and why, can be made clear by an understanding of the differences between family groups and juvenile peer-groups.

Family groups are not peer-groups. Their members are extremely heterogeneous. Families are organized to provide stable associations between young and old, between males and females, between the trained and the untrained, between the innocent and the sophisticated. Whether these differences are due to chronological age or to differences in previous experience and training, significant inequalities exist between members of families. If family groups are to fulfill the functions for which they are organized, they must be organized around clear divisions of labor and authority. What social and cultural elements families provide for their young and by what means, has been described in the discussion of the stages of infancy and childhood. Children live almost exclusively within the social boundaries of their families. If they lack families of their own, substitute families must be provided.[1] If they are not, children are seriously disadvantaged.

But family groups are limited in what they can do for children. Even corporate and extended families have very partial access to material, personal, and cultural resources in relation to the range of resources that constitute their societies. The resources of autonomous nuclear family groups—made up of husband, wife and their offspring—are extremely restricted. In any but tribal communities and agrarian, traditional societies in which corporate family organizations, usually called tribes or clans, control a large proportion of the cultural and material wealth of their societies, families are necessary but insufficient training groups for adult competence. They cannot prepare their young for life among strangers, or even, in the case of autonomous nuclear families, of life with equals. They cannot provide them with an adequate range of knowledge and skills. They do not prepare them for adult participation in the more complex organizations in their societies, or for coping with the heterogeneity, impersonality, and extreme differentiation of labor and authority that characterizes large modern industrial societies.

The development of the social abilities that are necessary to deal effectively with these social situations begins in juvenile peer-groups which are essentially oriented to the needs and interests of the juveniles themselves, not to their

[1] Community care of children in organizations such as the kibbutzim of Israel is, in effect, similar to child rearing in large, extended families, such as the traditional Chinese family.

families. Therefore, participation in them represents an extension of the social orbit that characterized childhood. Unlike family groups, these are peer-groups. Therefore, they provide very different services for their members.

Elders and authorities supply the young and uninitiated with satisfactions of many basic needs of the food, clothing, and shelter varieties. They may do this well or badly. They also provide knowledge, techniques, and equipment for many activities. Goods and services available are in their hands. What they cannot provide is the kind of relationship in which validation of experience and meanings of many kinds can be grounded. They can direct, they can correct, but the gap between the meanings of things and concepts and experience as conceived by the old and experienced and the young and inexperienced is great. The young and inexperienced acquire vocabularies and formulae, they emulate behavior, in some measure they witness and hear about birth and death and responsibilities for others and work and love and societies and countless other things, but ignorance and lack of actual experience of these makes what they see and hear mean something very different from what they mean to the older and experienced.

Furthermore, in the actual exercise of skills, direction and correction alone are insufficient. Competition can occur only between equals and competition is an important spur to the exercise of abilities and the acquisition of skills that are valued among the people among whom individuals live. The achievement of equal competence with elders requires exercise with peers along the way. Otherwise, prolonged incompetence in relation to superiors and the defeat guaranteed by the great inequality of skills and knowledge between the young and old, trained and untrained, is more likely to interfere with the acquisition of competence by the young and untrained than to foster it.

The acquisition of what most individuals come to accept as consensually valid meanings, or significance, or merely the facts of adult living, or of life in a particular organization, also requires some experience with peers. The young and inexperienced cannot come to these all at once, certainly not by merely being told about them by their elders or authorities. Their ultimate competence depends upon a great deal of communication between the young and inexperienced themselves. Juvenile peer-groups also develop the ability for competition and cooperation in their members. They expand skills and ability to regulate individual actions according to rules and norms, and develop capacity to deal with peers as necessary participants in a great many collective performances.

However, the interest of juveniles of any age does not extend beyond what each can contribute to the collective activity that is the means to what each needs or wants. Any peer who does not, or cannot, do this is dropped. Any peer who attempts to bring into the group situation individual concerns irrelevant to it is cautioned and, if that fails, excluded. The value of juvenile peers to one another is instrumental and rises in direct relation to skill at forwarding the collective action in which each is engaged for his own reasons.

Cultivation in juvenile peer-groups is even more specialized than that in family groups. They are organized for very particular ends. They are excellent arrangements for developing the knowledge and skills that lead to these ends because juvenile peers ruthlessly apply sanctions to anyone who fails to meet the standards of performance that their particular activities and membership rules demand. Juveniles are rigid conformists to juvenile rules.

There is a characteristic of juvenile peer-groups that is almost always unnoticed by their members. Because participation in these groups is the first experience of relatively stable associations with others separated from obvious observation and regulation by elders or superiors, it evokes a particularly keen aura of freedom from imposed constraints for juveniles. In fact, juvenile peer-groups are not autonomous. They continue to be dependent, not only for material means to achieve their ends, but for instruction and even some regulation. Rewards for achievement by these groups are also often in the hands of elders. Finally, in many instances, even membership in these groups is determined by authorities, not by the members themselves.

Most of the potential developments of the juvenile era, the outstanding characteristics of juveniles, their typical relations with one another, and the assets and liabilities of this phase of social development for collective life are well revealed in the athletic teams that are a conspicuous feature of the life of juveniles. Athletic teams are almost ideal-typical juvenile peer-groups. Since this form of organization is a powerful sociological device for achieving collective ends of all kinds as well as a potentially potent means for the social development of individuals, it is useful to summarize the juvenile era by analyzing it.

Membership on teams satisfies two vital juvenile needs, the need for association with peers and the need to cultivate and exercise abilities that cannot be developed outside social situations of relative equality. The membership is homogeneous with respect to the items of major interest to its individual constituents and it is usually voluntarily sought. For those who choose to seek it, making a team often seems a matter of life and death, a fact that reveals the strength of the individual needs involved.

The requisites for membership are clearly indicated and require considerable individual effort and self-regulation to acquire. Candidates go into training. They deny themselves all kinds of other satisfactions. They practice for hours over weeks and months, thereby cutting themselves off from others not similarly occupied. Although the skills and information cultivated are voluntarily pursued, their particular forms and the criteria of competence are established by authorities most of whom are in no direct association with the participants. Selection for membership depends upon coaches and the people behind them who make the organization of a team possible, not upon peers who, in the early stages of team life, are chiefly competitors. Performance is highly standardized. Individuals are not chosen for membership for being different from their rivals, only for being better at the same things.

Once a team is organized, voluntary cooperation between teammates is characteristic. Competition is reserved for associations with other teams. For team members the satisfactions provided by their selection are very great. They are assured of approval and acceptance by some peers. They can exercise skills that are important to them. Their homogeneity and equality greatly reduce the anxieties that are involved in competition and uncertainty about the approval of significant other people. The relief from this strain felt by new team members often results in a state that borders on euphoria. The individual importance of team membership is made manifest in taking on group insignia as personal traits and garments. These differentiate teammates from competitors and unimportant people and reinforce their exchanges with one another. The sources of strain in team life are chiefly connected with the maintenance of standards. Practice in comformity is intense.

That the conformity is to standards set up by remote others tends to escape attention. Rules are not questioned. Teams elect their captains and defer to their decisions. Captains represent their teammates in dealings with authorities and outsiders. The members have little to do with any factors that influence their team activities other than those involved in their own performances.

In no other social situation is virtue more its own reward than in teams. Team members "give their all" to the enterprise for the privilege of participating in it. Symbolic rewards in the form of a piece of felt or a button are more than adequate. The discipline of practice, injury, separation from other people and activities are scarcely noticed. The success of the team in competition with other teams dominates the individual interests of each member. Its achievement is their supreme satisfaction. The welfare of the team takes precedence over that of any individual on it.

This experience is positively ennobling, especially for chronological juveniles. For them, and also for adults whose social orientation remains essentially juvenile, this extraordinary limit to egocentrism is likely to be experienced as the ultimate in human altruism. Teammates usually believe that they are bound to one another for life. They think that they have intrinsic value to one another. In fact, they overestimate their attachments, but certainly the intrinsic value of their teams, if not their teammates, to juveniles is a large step beyond the egocentric adaptations to others among children. They are aware of something that transcends them and some people are viewed with great esteem for contributions to collective action as well as to their individual satisfactions.

The social limitations of juvenile associations are readily

apparent only to people who have moved beyond this stage of development. They are not likely to be noticed by teammates. In fact team membership requires that each individual eliminate all personal concerns that do not contribute to their skills and their teams. That a member of a basketball team may also be a good student is likely to be of only passing interest at best to his teammates. If he missed basketball practice in order to pursue his intellectual interests he would be censured. Yet the academic performance of a member that was falling below the level that is required for his participation on the team would immediately capture the attention of his teammates. Despite their feeling of intimacy, investigation of the relationships between teammates reveals that, unless they have developed into something else, they are remarkably impersonal. Teammates are extremely familiar with one another, but often very partially known outside of the narrow range of interests encompassed by team activities. Incidentally, this may equally be true of family members, as the derivation of the word "familiar" implies. These relationships can be satisfying and stable, but whether they are or not, depends upon their continued utility. If this ends, so do the relationships. Juveniles are "fair-weather" friends, which is to say, not friends at all.

Nevertheless, juvenile peer-groups are essential for the development of the potential social abilities of juveniles for the reasons indicated. They make juveniles aware, as children are not, of the meaning of membership requirements. Family membership is given to each individual and can be withdrawn only for very exceptional causes, no matter what his behavior. To quote Robert Frost: "Home is where, when you have to go there, they have to take you in." This is in no way true of juvenile peer-groups. Membership requires very precisely defined attributes and skills. Anyone who lacks them is excluded, no matter what other assets he may have. The rules are applied impersonally. Juvenile peers are much harder to manipulate and much less indulgent to one another than are family members and a good many other adults. This fact has several important consequences for their social development.

Because juveniles are intolerant of their peers' talk that is meaningless to them, they coerce them to make their language performance more precise. Because juvenile peers are eager to communicate with one another, they find that autistic verbiage is an impediment, and abandon it. Because these young people are peers, they are equally aware of their magical devices and will not put up with them. For example, a revival of a magical cry or phrase from infancy and childhood will not work. "Cry-babies" are not chosen as playmates. "I'm sorry" will not repeatedly excuse tardiness for the softball game. Therefore, these less mature social devices which may be tolerated by family members are eliminated by experience with peers. The importance to juveniles of membership in their peer-groups disposes them to meet the requirements for it. These include a large assortment of new cultural items: all kinds of physical skills, especially those required for games; systematic knowledge about all kinds of things such as cars, planes, animals, the way things work; acquaintance with and acceptance of the rules and codes that are associated with the group life of juveniles.

It is in the juvenile phase that elders usually introduce systematic formal education of the kind required for adult performance in the society. Because much of this is abstract, juveniles can do little more than rote learn it; they cannot comprehend it or grasp its ultimate significance. Because formal schooling, especially in modern, technological societies, is and must be geared to performance in what is for juveniles an inconceivably remote future, and because the utility of what is learned has little relevance for the immediate concerns of juveniles, few of them take to it with enthusiasm.

Those with special linguistic and conceptual abilities may find it fun, an exercise of ability. Some accept it with no protest as one of many incomprehensible demands of adults easier to adapt to than to avoid, especially if it leads to sensible and immediate rewards, like praise and prizes. For many juveniles some of the requirements of formal schooling are a burdensome imposition because they are beyond their actual capacities. When this is the case, personal disintegration, social regression, or rebellion often follow. In all cases, there are few juveniles who choose to spend their time in "book learning." The juvenile is a period of action. Juveniles "go reluctantly to school." Therefore, school life is full of coercions by adults; bribes for compliance, punishment for non-compliance. Cooperation with adults by juveniles is still chiefly related to their continued dependence upon them for essential satisfactions and, hence, the powers their elders have to coerce them.

In sharp contrast to this, compliance by juveniles to the demands of their peers is not only willingly granted, but is actively sought. For this reason what juvenile peer-groups can do in the way of social cultivation is so easily and effectively done. There are two principal coercions involved. The first is the great psychobiological need of juveniles for stable associations with their kind. The second is related to the first. Juvenile peers, unlike the elders responsible for juveniles, can refuse to include any one of them in their groups and can very easily expel a member who does not meet the group standards. In short, peers have the power of ostracism. It is a potent weapon and is, essentially, the weapon of equals.

The most conspicuous form of interaction among juveniles is competition. In the case of chronological juveniles, it is a new mode of exchange with others. The young cannot compete with adults. Their clamor and maneuvers for the attention of adults is frequently and erroneously referred to as competition. In the first dozen years of life, most siblings are not peers either, unless they are twins. Two years' difference in age, even one year's difference, represents too large a gap during the years of rapid growth. Siblings are not competing with one another when they demand at least equal and, more often, special consideration from others. Their goal is the elimination of an interference with access to what they want.

Competition is an advance in social skill in that it restrains this impulse to eliminate others.[2] Its manifestation is associated with the recognition that for some purposes the cooperation of others is not merely a necessity, a means to an end, but a source of satisfaction. For the

[2] Georg Simmel, in Nicholas Spykman, *The Social Theories of Georg Simmel* (New York: Atherton Press, 1966).

young, dependency on adults and their powers of coercion that follow from it, exclude this kind of cooperation with them. It is in play with their peers, and especially in games, that juveniles discover the satisfaction that can be derived from cooperation toward a commonly sought end. Their essential indifference to one another as persons enables them to contribute equally to the enterprise. Whatever the coercions that may be involved, they are equally available to each participant.

Competition is a form of interaction that is preeminently directed toward success in a particular kind of activity. Individuals compete for something specific. They are not interested in their rivals *per se*. The value of competitors is simply that one cannot demonstrate one's own abilities without them, cannot even enter into some activities without them. The elimination of a competitor before the competition defeats one's ends. These can only be served by being better than he is. In competition, rivals are only temporarily eliminated. They can lose in pursuit of success in a particular race, in winning a particular prize, but a social situation remains competitive only as long as contestants start as relative equals in each contest and each might win. If and when an individual can actually eliminate others from participation in an on-going activity, the social situation is one of conflict in pursuit of domination or elimination of the other. Activity that is sometimes described as "cut-throat competition" is not competition, it is conflict.

Juvenile activities thrive on competition. Juveniles cannot continue their games by eliminating their playmates. Recourse to conflict in pursuit of domination does not serve the ends of juveniles. It constitutes a "foul." Competition requires not only relative equality between participants, but rules and standardization of means to the ends sought and strict conformity to them among participants. Therefore, difference and originality are not juvenile traits. They do not lead to success among juveniles of any chronological age. Acceptance among them depends upon likeness: of traits, of skills, of interests. A conception of equality that is not based on uniformity is beyond them, a fact that exposes their essential disinterest in one another as intrinsically valuable beings.

Juvenile peer groups are conspicuously homogeneous. The power of ostracism employed by juvenile peers keeps them so. Acceptance depends on the acquisition of particular attributes and ability for particular performance. Continued participation depends upon maintaining both at standard levels. Exclusion deprives juveniles of what they need most: access to their peers and the opportunities these provide for the cultivation and exercise of their abilities. Ostracism by one's kind is a social equivalent of physical death. For juveniles, their kind is a very limited category of the human race. Their tolerance for people who differ from them is extremely limited. It is juvenile peer-groups that manifest what sociologists have labeled strong "in-group" and "out-group" sentiments in their most fully developed forms.

The ability that can be cultivated in juveniles to operate as effective and efficient units in groups to achieve goals that can only be accomplished by collective efforts takes them a long way toward mature social competence. In this respect it is a great advance over childhood.

The negotiation of the potentialities of the juvenile stage of development cultivates social skills in individuals that are far more useful for collective life than those that characterize children. The need for relationships with equals evokes voluntary cooperation. Among juveniles, competition replaces attempts to eliminate others, the criterion of competence as a requisite for personal satisfactions is accepted, the experience of delegated authority changes responses to authority in general, and deference to it expands the social areas of autonomy for juveniles. The discovery that particular collective arrangements can be the source of great individual satisfactions leads to the appearance of willingness to make individual resources available for collective ends for little in the way of reward from outsiders.

Adult life can be lived on a fairly complex level with no more than the resources of juveniles, and much of it is. Family groups tend to limit impulses for voluntary cooperation to people related by kinship or on whom family welfare depends. Juvenile peer-groups extend this cooperation to strangers, so long as they are not significantly different. Family groups are dominated by elders who can choose to be indulgent or demanding, forgiving or punitive. The extension of family patterns to other spheres of life takes the form of authoritarian control or patronage. But juvenile peer-groups can develop the techniques of political democracy. They cultivate relationships of equality, decision by majority vote, the delegation of authority, and deference to it. They distribute place and rewards on the basis of skill and competence rather than on birth or position in a hierarchy. Emphasis on the acquisition of skill develops attitudes and personal habits that are useful for the development and maintenance of complex technology and the organizations that these require. In short, the realization of the social potentialities of juveniles moves the actually young a long way toward competent adult life, even as citizens of complex societies. It falls considerably short of the whole way, however.

Juveniles of any age live by codes and the letter is often confused with the spirit of laws and regulations about which juveniles know very little. They are literal people. Social situations tend to seem more simple than they are to juveniles. They are likely to be satisfied with slogans and stereotypes. They are impatient with abstract analysis and open-ended questions.

For people who lack the experience and conviction of the intrinsic worth of others, everyone, including themselves, continues to be experienced as instrumental. Also, for them, only the cultural forms that are widely supported by the exercise of sanctions by useful people are important guides for action. These are, I suppose, Riesman's "other-directed" people.[3] They experience cultural prescriptions much as they did as children, that is, as arbitrary impositions that, for reasons unknown, must be followed to achieve satisfaction and avoid dissatisfaction. According to Piaget, causal connections are neither sought nor expressed before seven to eight years of age. Some people never seek them.

The persistent need for approval from peers and for membership in peer-groups makes a juvenile way of life

[3] David Riesman. *The Lonely Crowd* (New Haven: Yale University Press, 1950).

vulnerable to considerable anxiety. The discomfort evoked by people who are different can be escaped by the practice of techniques of social avoidance. But the anxiety evoked by the withdrawal of support by peers, or the loss of peers in later life through death and dispersion, cannot. Juveniles do not escape life on an anxiety gradient. They are under continuous strain to meet and maintain particular standards. The proverbial "Joneses" and the people who must "keep up" with them are adult juveniles.

When attention is principally absorbed in checking on the immediate utility of people, culture and things, there is little energy left for spontaneity and improvisation. For people for whom others remain instrumental, a sharp division between means and ends tends to be maintained. In consequence, they are not likely to reach gratifying ends and tend to push on and on in their search for satisfaction. There is always a race to be won, and winning does not bring satisfaction for long. Visible symbols of success are the only assurance that they have succeeded and these must keep coming, hence the next race. Juveniles of all ages are vastly concerned with status, prestige, success, etc., and the external indices thereof. Yet, even when they achieve them they are restless and their own fairly constant activity is often referred to as a "rat-race." Of the cultural realm, only the practical or diverting elements interest them.

Because the effects of ultimate authority are frequently mediated for juvenile types while they are more often in direct contact only with their selected leaders, juveniles are apt to accept authority as relatively benign. They tend to be "good citizens" unless conditions throw them into contact with the new and different, which sometimes turns them malevolent. But they are more likely to contribute to the stability of their social orders and the maintenance of the status quo. Whether or not this is an asset to them and the populations in which they live depends upon whether or not the authority is in fact benign and the status quo does in fact provide adequately for the maintenance of a population.

Adult juveniles do not initiate change or adapt to it easily unless they are manipulated by authorities who can provide them with immediate gratifications and who define the proposed changes in terms that do not run counter to their established convictions. But leaders of social movements often mobilize them to serve their own ends without revealing what these are. Organizations for social change usually consist of a series of juvenile-type peer-groups or teams that serve authoritarian leaders with whom they have little or no contact. The participants feel that they are carrying out programs vital to their own needs under leaders of their own choosing.[4] In ordinary circumstances, juvenile peer-type groups are used in schools, churches, and other large organizations to promote their programs and encourage continued proficiency in whatever it is they require from their members. The organization of memberships into teams in competition with one another for small prizes is still as good a way to promote scholarship, get money for a new church organ, cut down damage to equipment in a factory, or fill the community chest as any.

For all these reasons, it is apparent that, useful though they are, the accomplishments of juveniles are not sufficient for the achievement and maintenance of many individual adult satisfactions, nor is this level of social development a dependable basis for the stability and successful operation of complex social orders. If individuals are fairly fortunate, their experiences as juveniles and their own psychobiological maturation open up new social possibilities. The transition from the juvenile to the preadolescent stage of social development is indicated when a juvenile begins to view one of his group-mates as more significant than the others, not merely because of his contributions to the group, but simply by virtue of what he is as a person. Pairings between some group-mates become noticeable. They are often resented by the rest who quite rightly suspect that the allegiance to their groups of the participants in these pairs is waning.

This is the beginning of a capacity for friendship. It marks the beginning of the end of the essential egocentricity with which all human beings begin life and many end it.

---

[4] There is an excellent example of this kind of organization in Mu Fu-Sheng, *The Wilting of the Hundred Flowers* (New York: Praeger, 1963).

With the acquisition of a friend, a young person experiences another individual as having as much importance as he has to himself. For the first time the satisfaction of the needs of another becomes as important as the satisfaction of his own. The transcendence of peer-groups is replaced by the transcendence of some particular people.

Juvenile peer groups train individuals for membership in particular organizations, for living with particular kinds of people. Friendship can, with luck, lead to the ability to live comfortably with a wide variety of mankind. The experience of friendship can be generalized into a sense of humanity, something quite different from partisanship.

Chapter Five

Pre-adolescence

THE SOCIAL DEVELOPMENT of greatest importance in pre-adolescence is the appearance of capacity for viewing some particular other people as possessed of intrinsic worth. More simply, pre-adolescence is distinguished by the development of the capacity for friendship. This is the first move away from essential egocentricity and toward ability for fully responsible associations with other people because they are experienced as something more than sources of individual satisfactions and dissatisfactions.

This phase has been largely overlooked by social scientists. Harry Stack Sullivan is the only one I know who differentiated it from others in the developmental sequence. The oversight is understandable. Nothing conspicuous is added to the biological resources of pre-adolescents. They do not even manifest any great strides in perceptual and motor skills, as juveniles do. Their new asset is the beginning of ability for abstract thought, and this is not directly observable. It is a capacity that varies greatly among any particular population, even a pre-adolescent one. Aside from the probability of some differences between individuals in innate potential for this kind of activity, it seems to depend in large measure on the successful cultivation of the resources of earlier development. Certainly the achievement of consistent competence in handling abstractions, and especially their effective application to empirical experience, takes a great deal more cultivation. But the potential for this is available in many human beings around the ages of ten or eleven and it is this that marks the psychobiological boundary of pre-adolescence and is the basis for the social developments that characterize it.

It should be needless to say that aging alone in no way guarantees effective use of this potential. In fact, by the time chronological pre-adolescence is reached, there is a great discrepancy between the somatic and social development of many young people, which, in the case of a large proportion of these, is not overcome in their lifetime. Many physically adult people are essentially childish in social terms and juvenile social skills represent very considerable achievement for collective living and suffice for many adults. It should be apparent that there are so many factors involved in social development that are neither biologically nor socially controlled, nor controllable, that the odds are against a large proportion of human beings living out anything like the full range of their psychobiological potential. Fortunately, it appears that they have not needed to for their survival as a species. However, the contribution to the universe of the realm of social and cultural phenomena by human beings has been an outcome of their mental abilities. The development of these to a level of abstract thinking in a significant number of each generation of human beings has been essential for this. It is also essential for the full development of individual lives.

Typically, ability for abstract thought begins in pre-adolescence. If the resources of the juvenile period are successfully negotiated, pre-adolescents have an extensive reservoir of validated concepts and words with which they have differentiated the items of the concrete world and of visible action with considerable precision. Based on this, they have formulated a large number of useful empirical generalizations. The next step is generalization of non-material aspects of the universe: qualities, relationships, the nature of thought itself and its products, the non-material properties of physical things, and so on. All of this begins when the power of abstract thought becomes available. It can only be achieved if it is extensively developed.

The ability for abstract thought, which includes operations such as inference, deduction, induction, analysis and synthesis, is as necessary for understanding the intrinsic nature of human beings as it is for grasping the nature of other phenomena. Until it is available, other people can be identified as entities, sorted according to a variety of criteria relevant to the sorter, and used in a great number of ways, but they cannot be understood. Recognition that other people have needs and sensations and impulses and conditions like, or similar, to one's own, depends upon clear formulation of one's own states, inferences about theirs, and ability for dependable communication. No one directly shares the pain, pleasure, joy, or sorrows of another. Whether or not an individual even believes that other people have them depends on his achieving a high level of social development. "No one knows the trouble I have," "No one knows my pain," "No one has suffered as I have" are common complaints and most of the people who make them believe they are true. The other fellow's case, whatever it is, is different.

In the absence of ability to infer or be informed of the states of others, their significance perforce remains attached to their impact on oneself. They may be highly regarded, respected for their obvious skills, accomplishments, and ability to provide services and satisfactions, but their right to exist, so to speak, or at least their right to consideration, rests on their performances, not on their sheer existence. They may be useful, or unavoidable, but they have nothing like one's intrinsic value to oneself.

Egocentricity can only be breached by the mind, the body will never transcend it. Everyone starts life totally dominated by somatic needs and conditions. Limitation and regulation of somatic impulse depend upon helplessness, or external restraint, until unnoticed "conditioning" or "imprinting" modifies somatic function and mental activities evolve to regulate behavior by conceptual interferences with organic impulse. The latter is what is meant by "self-regulation." It is greatly advanced when conceptual abilities are advanced.

The giant stride in conceptual skills that occurs in preadolescence results in two major social developments. For the first time, the young begin to move out of the essential egocentricity with which everyone begins life. Their biological impulses begin to be dominated by the conceptual content of the "mind," and, for the first time, some particular other persons are recognized as intrinsically valuable and interesting as people at least almost as important as themselves. Pre-adolescents acquire friends.

Friendship is characterized by its remarkable freedom from association with particular performances, particular rules, particular personal attributes, particular sets of sanctions. The limitation of experience and conceptual capacity in early pre-adolescence directs initial impulses toward friendship to a person of the same sex and approximately of the same age and interests. It is easier to notice that another person is experiencing life much as one does oneself if he or she is like one in important respects. But these initial explorations, if not impeded or damaged, result in personal developments that make it possible to view a great many people as being at least as human as oneself. It then follows that they are worthy of respect and entitled to what they need and want to develop their resources and satisfy their needs. Further, the ability to supply these satisfactions to them becomes a source of individual, personal satisfaction in itself.

This "satisfaction in giving satisfaction," as H. S. Sullivan called it, usually first experienced in relation to a friend though its roots may lie in the "satisfaction response" of infancy, is actually an addition to the category of motives that impel individuals to act in their characteristic ways. It is entirely a product of experience with other people of a particular kind, not of cultural modification. It is not to be confused with the desire to please in order to win approval or particular attentions, or to avoid disapproval and unpleasant consequences, that are typical of children and juveniles. Neither should it be confused with notions of sacrifice or selflessness. On the contrary, it is a great source of individual satisfaction because the intrinsic value of the persons whose needs one wishes to satisfy makes them extensions of one's own.

This is remarkable social achievement, something that is not possible on the somatic level alone. In fact, it is a powerful limitation on somatic impulse to absolute satisfactions. It is a social motive that, like all social development, interferes with raw organic impulse. Once individuals experience it, always in relations with particular other people initially, even the curtailment of biological gratifications, such as food, clothing, sleep and so forth, if this is necessary to enable a person to provide for someone he intrinsically values, is literally not important. He is more than compensated by his satisfaction in giving satisfaction. No sacrifice is involved because there is no lack of gratification. It is simply that the gratification is an enhancement of self-esteem rather than the satisfaction of organic needs and wants. It is a kind of satisfaction that is almost impossible to explain to people who have not undergone the transformations of pre-adolescence.

Recognition of the intrinsic value of another person refers to a relationship of intimacy which must be distinguished from mere familiarity. Intimacy implies that the parties involved are of equal worth to each other because otherwise extensively uncensored communication is out of the question. Just what determines the establishment of these most durable of human associations we do not know. Nevertheless, the acceptance of each participant by the other without special qualifications, by removing the anxiety that constant appraisal in terms of approval and disapproval for specific performances and dependency for particular services evoke, encourages the formulations of all the experience of each friend for communication to the other. Friends discuss a wider range of things with each other than they do in any other association, including, or possibly especially, family relationships. This act of communication brings each one's experience more clearly and firmly into his own awareness. It also reveals new aspects of the human condition while it confirms the fact that others share one's own.

Discovery of essential similarities that are not obvious creates a sense of belonging to mankind, of sharing a common lot. This is a necessary basis for what is called "a sense of humanity." The recognition that some others are essentially like oneself coupled with new conceptual abilities leads to a generalization about mankind. Very few others are viewed as extensions of self, but for people who have friends few others can be viewed as things, mere instruments for the achievement of particular ends. This discovery also relieves each individual from the sense of uniqueness that is fostered by physical separateness and that is the burden of the young, immature, and mentally ill. The talk of friends usually leads to an exchange of confidences which include the record of lapses from approved behavior or sentiments. The discovery that a highly valued other person also stole cookies from the cookie jar, indulged in erotic fantasies, and entertained some unflattering sentiments about his mother de-fuses great loads of anxiety and enhances self-esteem. The fact that these revelations do not threaten the relationship adds immensely to personal security.

Friendship transcends kinship as well as team-type memberships in that both of these are freighted with rights, obligations, and practical utility. Relatives and teammates may come to be invested with the quality of attachment (love, perhaps) we call friendship, but until and unless they are, their instrumental aspects limit them as comfortable extensions of oneself, for this, in ways still unexplained, is what friends become. Friendship is the way out of loneliness, which can be experienced in the presence of others. It is a kind of permanent attachment experienced as something like an energy hook-up and it operates even when the other is not physically present. If one has friends one is not "lonely in a crowd." Moreover, one is not lonely in one's family circle.

The sense of one's own intrinsic worth that is derived from a friend's appraisal is different from the sense of acceptability that follows from approval for specific performances which characterize successful children and juveniles. With friends there is no apprehension of rejection in the absence of ability to meet particular standards. Occasions for anxiety are greatly reduced.

Self-esteem is essential to any favorable view of mankind. No one who conceives of himself as hateful, largely incompetent, unacceptable, can see another differently. No one whose self-respect depends upon continuous manifestations of approval for performance can be comfortable with his fellows. Many such people learned as early as the age of three what words to say, what gestures to make, and under what circumstances it is wise to use them. These magical devices, if encouraged by elders whose abilities for relationship are limited, leave the child-grown-adult with a pretty poor opinion of people and himself. Even if he has successfully deflected his attention from his essentially dramatic impersonations, the fraud involved is not a secure way of life. Dis-ease does not make for intimacy with others and thus prevents escape from the anxiety gradient with which everyone must cope in early life and the concomitant achievement of the expansion of personal abilities that intimacy brings. It very frequently leads to disease. This is the fallacy in the assumption that competent development and personal integration equates with the acquisition of skills for role-playing. Role-playing is not enough for mature social competence.

Because roles represent divisions of labor and authority associated with prerequisites for membership in organizations and connected with requirements for their maintenance, they do not provide cues about the intrinsic worth of individuals. The responses of people in role associations with one another depend upon the extent to which they meet the impersonal standards involved in the particular membership requirements. The maintenance of the association depends upon fulfilling expectations. Therefore, personal differences that interfere with this fulfillment make individuals unacceptable. Their intrinsic worth is not involved. Anyone who can meet the role requirements better can replace a defaulting member.

This is not the case in associations between people who have personal significance for one another, let alone for those who recognize their intrinsic value. For these particular people take precedence over their competence or incompetence as role-players in groups and other organizations. In friendships people discover that difference can be neutral, that it does not automatically imply worthlessness. Friends respect one another's interests, explore them, and so expand their own. Extension of the limits of early enculturation in families and play groups is most easily achieved by people who have friends. Tolerance for social heterogeneity depends upon the discovery of the intrinsic worth of some particular other people. This is one of the greatest differences between juveniles and pre-adolescents of any chronological age. Equality comes to mean common humanity, not a matching of physical and social and cultural traits.

One result of this is a great extension of the cultural

repertoire of pre-adolescents. What friends do most with each other is talk. Their new-found significance to each other evokes the impulse to communicate their experiences, their states of being, their evolving thoughts. In this exchange language is enhanced and referents become more precise. The consensual validation of meaning, of words and experience, is substantially augmented.

With the reduction in threats of anxiety that is characteristic of associations between people who have intrinsic value for one another, the participants are free to exercise their curiosity and to explore the cultural resources available to them as juveniles explore the physical environment around them. The new conceptual resources of pre-adolescents enable them to do so.

The rote-learning and emulation of children and juveniles are not enough for the acquisition of a large and varied cultural repertoire and its effective use for individual and collective maintenance and development. Learning must be recognized as an implementation of individual resources that makes for competence in living. It is in the interpersonal experience of pre-adolescents that individuals begin to discern this. When they do, "culture" comes to be seen as something more than an arbitrary intrusion between need and satisfaction made by elders and authorities. In school, for burgeoning pre-adolescents, some teachers become mentors, sources of information and advice that is sought by them. Mentors are authorities to whom the young defer rather than submit because associations with them provide exciting insights into themselves and others and glimpses of the variety and complexity of the world beyond their immediate experience.[1]

Although friends do not usually employ the coercions used by others in their relations with them on each other, friendship develops a response to others that is itself coercive, namely, sympathy. What is referred to here must be distinguished from what has been described as "empathy," though the words are sometimes used as synonyms.

[1] "The Rainmaker," in Hermann Hesse's *Magister Ludi* (New York: Ungar) is an excellent illustration of the reciprocities between a mentor and his students and the potentialities for his exploitation by those to whom he is simply an instrument.

Empathy is essentially pre-conceptual and undifferentiated. Its impact results in a kind of total state of the organism that is neither identified nor subject to regulation. Sympathy, on the contrary, depends upon conceptual powers. It implies that the state of another has been investigated and formulated. Sympathy, as used here, is the ability to take the place of another. It is not, incidentally, the special instance of shared sentiment implied in common usage, such as the "I sympathize with you in the death of your near and dear" sort of thing, which may be an instance of sympathy, but which may be a pure case of the magical use of words.

George Mead[2] based his theory of the development of self and of social traits on the child's "taking the place of the other," on the capacity of human beings for sympathy. In my opinion, he was correct in noting the fact that this has a coercive effect on individuals. If one actually identifies the state of another, one is likely to react to it. It is difficult to treat people as things, or merely instruments, once one has become clearly aware of the fact that everyone is trapped in what has been called "the human condition." But I think that Mead's assumption that the capacity for sympathy is inherent in human beings or available in early life is wrong. Only the potential for it is inherent and it requires conceptual ability that is not usually available until ten or eleven and must be cultivated thereafter. It is available for most human beings at pre-adolescence. Whether or not it is manifest by adults depends upon their having successfully negotiated this stage of development.

Friendship introduces a new form of interaction to the participants which I, following H. S. Sullivan's terminology, call collaboration. Collaboration can only occur between people who are very extensively self-regulated and who trust each other. It depends on neither coercion nor similarity of skills and resources. Equality, for collaborators, resides in mutual intrinsic value, not in a careful balance of assets and liabilities. Therefore, collaboration is not a form of interaction available to infants, children, or juveniles. It

[2] George Mead, *Mind, Self and Society* (Chicago: University of Chicago Press, 1946).

implies a responsiveness to the needs of others, as well as one's own, and recognition of the validity of interests and standards other than one's own. Concern for the satisfaction of the needs of others imposes restraint upon one's own strivings for satisfaction. Collaboration is self-regulated activity that does not require the threat of coercion or the promise of gratification to sustain. Collaborators do not take egocentric advantage of each other, even when the opportunity for so doing exists. The intrinsic significance of each to the other and their satisfaction in giving satisfaction are its positive supports.

Since Charles Cooley introduced the concept "primary" to differentiate associations between people that cultivate their essential personal traits and skills from those that merely provide information or routine assistance, it has been generally assumed by social scientists that all participants in "primary" relationships view each other as having "intrinsic" worth. That they consider each other important is certain. But if the word "intrinsic" is taken as an antonym of "instrumental" and to refer to recognition of value that is independent of particular standards as well as use, then it is clear that the "primary" relationships of infants, children and juveniles do not involve their recognition of the intrinsic value of others and that there are more adults in any population who do not recognize it than there are those who do. The term refers to an acceptance of the sheer existence of someone without need for its justification on the basis of special qualifications, especially of their utility as means to ends that are of no concern to them. The application of the word "intrinsic" to people is not different from its application to objects classified as "art" in contrast to those classified as "tools." There are more skilled users of tools among adults than there are connoisseurs of art.

The great significance of pre-adolescent social development is precisely that it fosters the ability to recognize "intrinsic" worth. This is not only manifest in the friendships of pre-adolescents, but in their formation of groups, some of them primary groups, that differ in important ways from family groups and juvenile peer groups. Because these are especially characterized by the fact that their members do view one another as intrinsically worthy, I call them "intrinsic peer groups."

These are peer groups, but at this level of socialization, equality is not construed as homogeneity. Therefore, they are more useful than either family or juvenile groups for organizing people who differ in important traits such as race, education, or enculturation. These are voluntary and autonomous groups and are far fewer in number in any population than either of the other types. Pre-adolescents are not driven by a need for group membership *per se.* They tend to satisfy their need for peers in paired relationships. Therefore, when they organize into groups they do so for the achievement of particular ends which require more than two people and for which available organizations do not provide.

These are pre-eminently organizations for improvisation. Their personal significance to their members lies in their assistance in the development of special skills, or the discovery of something new, or opportunity to exercise abilities that are uncommon in a particular population. They facilitate communication between people who are becoming, or are, highly individuated and who, therefore, are likely to be excluded from juvenile groups.

Intrinsic peer groups are based on friendship. Recruitment is largely dependent upon the recommendation of one friend by another. Although most of the members of these groups have joined because they share a common interest and therefore manifest some similar personal traits, these groups often include what may be called marginal people who are interested friends rather than skilled participants. This does not mean that each member is in a friendship relationship with all others, only that each is usually a friend to some other and that mutual respect characterizes all associations in the group.

Intrinsic peer groups are ephemeral more often than not. Since it is people and the pursuit of special goals that has intrinsic value for their members, not grouping itself, once the ends for which these groups are organized are achieved, or routine means to these ends appear, these groups are dissolved. It is the friendships between members that persist.

The groups of chronological pre-adolescents who have

also achieved social pre-adolescence rarely survive for long. But the ability for collaboration, in contrast to competition and cooperation, in a group context that they cultivate is a socially valuable resource for adult life. Adult intrinsic peer groups are a major source of innovation for societal populations and of opportunity for creative activity for individuals. Furthermore, pre-adolescents of any age are sufficiently free from anxiety to pursue their ends without finding it necessary to impose them on people who differ from them. They can disagree without denigrating their opponents. They are not partisans. They are not competitive. They do not need continuous assurances of approval to bolster their self-esteem. Therefore, they can proceed on what may turn out to be a revolutionary course for the area of their interest without disrupting routine collective arrangements in their field.

An example of such a group and such an outcome is the group of painters called "The Batignolles." It included Monet, Renoir, Sisley, Pissarro, Cezanne, Degas, and Manet. It arose because of their individual experiments with new painting techniques which detached them from the studios of their day and, later, because of their exclusion from official salons. Over a number of years they collaborated with one another in the development of their skills and in the organization of their exhibitions. They also befriended one another in need. Some of them lived and prospered beyond the days of their exclusion. The group broke up when the need for it passed; the bonds between most of the artists did not.[3]

It was not "The Batignolles" who rioted in the art world. Adults who organize groups in the name of whatever cause to prevent others from pursuing their own, use the techniques of juvenile peer groups not intrinsic peer groups. They are intensely partisan and exclusive. In the name of freedom and equality they demand agreement with their

[3] "The Batignolles: Creators of Impressionism" by Maria Rogers in the *Autonomous Groups Bulletin*, Vol. IV, Nos. 3 and 4. Another example reported in the same issue is an article by Charles Kitzen called "The Old Gang, Nucleus of Fabianism," which describes the vital contribution of a group made up of Shaw, the Webbs, Wells and Oliver, among others, to Fabianism and the British Labour Party.

philosophies and goals. Difference is intolerable to them and they feel entirely justified in suppressing all who manifest it because they do not consider them to be fully human.

Most adult juvenile peer groups support collective order. Juveniles are conformist for the most part. But a combination of juvenile social orientation with the biological strivings and abstract conceptual flights that characterize adolescents often turns these groups into potent agents of division and destruction of collective life. The developments of pre-adolescence that transform passionate allegiance to groups into sympathetic concern for particular individuals, whether like oneself or not, provide a brake for the potential social misuse of juvenile skills.

It is difficult to convey the very great social significance of the developments in personal social skill that we call preadolescence. They are not conspicuous, being largely sociopsychological rather than physiological. They seem to be rooted physiologically chiefly in an increase in capacity for abstract conceptualization and the more complex and competent mental activities that follow from this. The great social change in pre-adolescence is the move away from the egocentricity of earlier stages toward a fully developed ability for intrinsic relationships with other people.

Recognition of the intrinsic aspects of human relationships, coupled with clear awareness of the on-going interdependence of people for the achievement of their satisfactions and security, makes people dependable social units. When they participate in instrumental groups and relations, such as work groups and professional relationships, their contribution of relevant and sufficient actions will rest on satisfaction in giving satisfaction to others as well as to the particular satisfactions that the situation provides. People who have negotiated the developments of pre-adolescence do not require, as do juvenile and childish people, clear indication of particular satisfactions or threat of uncomfortable coercions or deprivations to elicit their contributions to collective endeavors. These people tend to see what are called "culture" and "society" as instruments for human living created by human beings and valuable only insofar as they support and cultivate human beings.

At the same time, they recognize that, in general, relatively stable relationships and organizations and cultural determinants of arrangements for living are necessary for the survival, cultivation, and maintenance of human beings. Therefore, they are disposed to accept the limitations on their impulses that these impose, so long as they do not see them as crippling or lethal, and to contribute their energies and abilities to maintain and augment them. It is in this sense that the experience of pre-adolescence opens the way to a fully social way of life. A fairly competent grasp of the nature of human beings and of themselves that intimate relationships develop commits individuals not only to one another, but to the collective instruments that are the unique requirements of human beings.

The conceptual skills of these people are greatly augmented by their communication in relatively anxiety-free relationships. The new and the different become tolerable to them and so they are released from the need for excessive conformity to limited standards that characterizes juveniles. This enlightenment also involves the development of mental abilities to the point at which the mental integration of experience begins to take precedence over the somatic integration of experience, at least under ordinary circumstances. Conceptual regulation of organic dynamisms becomes habitual, a development that is 180 degrees from the situation in which everyone begins life. Most of this regulation works so smoothly that it scarcely evokes attention. But, in or out of awareness, conceptual interference with organic, egocentric impulses *is* self-regulation and it is the recognition of the intrinsic worth of some particular other people that begins in pre-adolescence that greatly augments the basis for it.

It must be clear by now that, since somatic growth guarantees nothing in the way of social developments, a given adult population (except unusual and deliberately selected ones) will include people who are very different in their actual abilities for maintaining relationships and contributing to collective enterprises. Their acquaintance with norms, skills and knowledge, etc., alone will not enable one to predict how people will perform in collective action: whether or not they will be "responsible," under what cir-

cumstances they will be dependable as social units, whether
or not they can be left to their own devices to accomplish
what they are assigned to do, whether or not they are capable of intimacy, what forms of organization will induce
them to keep their skills available for collective production
and maintenance.

It is the recognition that people have intrinsic, as well as
instrumental, value and, hence, that one has intrinsic value
also, that transforms individuals into dependable and competent social units in any of a wide range of social relationships, organizations, and activities. Extensive enculturation
alone will not do so. It is the social development in direct
relation with other people to a level on which individuals
voluntarily limit their impulses to exclusive satisfactions on
behalf of others in and for themselves, whatever their culture and utility, that is an essential mark of social maturity,
at least from a sociological point of view. Pre-adolescence is
the final step that opens the way to this achievement.

The negotiation of the pre-adolescent stage of social
development is a kind of watershed in the sphere of interpersonal relations. The way to it is long and complicated
and many people miss it. For those who do, other people
remain primarily sources of gratification or frustration. For
those who achieve pre-adolescent social skills, other people
are regarded as friendly or neutral at the least. At best they
view others as people essentially like themselves whatever
their culturally significant differences. Some others are
experienced as being as important as themselves. Once this
occurs the essential egocentricity that characterizes the
early stages of life for all human beings is breached. The
way to a fully social life is opened.

This is a highly desirable base from which to weather the
strains of the next stage of development because adolescence crashes in on everyone whether or not they are
socially ready for it. Competent pre-adolescents are the
most likely to benefit from its opportunities and to avoid
its dangers.

Chapter Six

Adolescence

THE SOCIAL STAGE of adolescence is remarkably conspicuous to everyone, everywhere, except, perhaps, to adolescents themselves who often assume they have reached maturity. Adolescence is made especially notable by the profusion of physiological developments that characterize it and their social consequences. It begins with the onset of puberty with its blossoming secondary sex characteristics that drastically alter the relationships of the young to one another and to everyone else. It initiates capacity for reproduction. Its principal biological strivings are for the stabilization of sexual function, the satisfaction of lust, and the achievement of stable interpersonal relationships for so doing. Its outcome is parenthood and the establishment of new nuclear family units, a result which is often unintended by adolescents themselves but which is encouraged by the cultural demands of their elders.

The biological fertility that is announced by the puberty change has evoked more comment than the appearance of secondary sex characteristics. It is, of course, the crux of the matter. But, in fact, the reproductive functions are not immediately stabilized or put to use in most instances and in most societies these physiological processes are banished from public performance and public comment. However, the cultural formulations about sex and reproduction used by adults to restrict sexual impulse and the relationships in which it can be legitimately satisfied are numerous among all people, and they are transmitted to the young with the strongest anxiety enforcement long before the latter have any use for them.

Consequently, sexual development and function are

hedged in by more magical words and rituals than any other physiological process. Few people reach adolescence without apprehension induced by the vague pronouncements of adults and older youths, or with precise information about what is happening to them physiologically, let alone socially. Because the physiological development occurs so late in life, the cultural intrusions supplied by elders between lust and its satisfaction are numerous, elaborate, and strongly bolstered by the threat of extreme anxiety in the absence of conformity to them. Anxiety always deflects attention away from its source. Therefore, between the cultural formulations that demand suppression and repression of sexual impulse and, at the very least, its direction into limited and specific social channels, and the anxiety evoked by the uncertainties that the biological facts of sex itself arouse, it is possible for young people to go through physical adolescence driven by impulses they know little about and ignorant about both the physiological and social aspects of sex. Because conceptual regulation of biological impulse is already highly developed by the time most individuals reach adolescence, it is possible for them to avoid the anxiety that adolescence evokes for them by withdrawing from the relationships that can stimulate and satisfy sexual impulse and defend their social position by elaborate cultural rationalizations. It is even possible for some of these people to reach the end of their lives with their defenses intact.

All this creates the paradox that the psychobiological additions that characterize adolescence include impulses that are among the most compelling that people experience; at the same time, they are the most likely to be frustrated by the cultural demands associated with them. Where the cultural formulations about sex are elaborate, as they are in Western European culture areas, for example, the intricacy of the path that leads to satisfaction is so great and the anxiety that deviations from it evoke so onerous, that a great many adults fail to reach competent sexual function at all and more fail to experience sexual satisfaction even though their physiological apparatus works.

Freudian theory is based on this social and cultural invasion of biological structure and function. Freud recognized the non-organic source of many of the organic difficulties suffered by the people who came to him. In my opinion, his explanation of them exaggerates the extent and importance of lust, or at least fails to differentiate it from other sensual satisfactions and underestimates the social and cultural factors involved. This invasion of the sexual apparatus and its function is no different from the modifications of gastro-intestinal structure and function that make some foods digestible and some not—a fact that is clearly illustrated by people raised in orthodox religions with rigid dietary laws—or that determines posture, gait, gesture, or the ability to hear and pronounce sound patterns.

The consequences of cultural interference with sexual function are somewhat different, however, because these physiological functions are available only long after conceptual abilities are well developed and, therefore, attention cannot be totally deflected from them. By the time infants and children and juveniles are able conceptually to identify their gastro-intestinal systems, or their skeletons and musculature, the basic socially induced cultural modifications of these that are deemed desirable by the people among whom they live have been integrated into them. But the physiological changes of adolescence come after many years of life. They are not gradual and they compel attention that no amount of previous enculturation and current anxiety can totally eliminate. This can drive the most anxious into catatonia or schizophrenia, in which states they block awareness of themselves; but they are so driven just because they could not avoid initial recognition of physiological impulse and could not find their way through their particular social and cultural maze to satisfy it.

Most people have not suffered such extreme social and cultural interference with regard to sexual processes and performance. But since none escape some from the past and, in most societies, a good deal during adolescence, and because they are quite capable of identifying their needs, they fight for their satisfactions. We have noted before that human beings do not willingly accept interference with compelling biological impulses. Coercions must be applied to achieve this from the beginning. Fortunately for mankind, though sometimes to the misfortune of particular individuals, infants and children, and even juveniles, have few means to resist coercions by their elders, they remain too dependent upon them for survival and maintenance, and it is perhaps fortunate for each of us that we lack the conceptual resources to know what is happening to us. But these fortunate conditions do not obtain for adolescents or for their elders. Hence, there is some inescapable conflict between them. How much depends upon how successfully the developments of earlier stages have been negotiated, the nature of the relevant cultural formulations, and the ease of access to the interpersonal arrangements that adolescent resources require for their development and satisfaction. It also depends upon the power of elders over adolescents, which in this period is chiefly the control of access to what adolescents need and want materially. In adolescence, the effect of people and their cultural means for maintenance on biological organisms is vividly revealed.

The strains of adolescence are not located entirely in the relationships between adolescents and the adults around them. Some of them stem from their physical and psychological condition itself. The suddenness of their growth at this time and its extent are a kind of invasion itself. Aside from the functions initiated by puberty, adolescents suffer sudden conspicuous changes in height, in weight, in skeletal structure. Males acquire beards and their voices change dramatically. Females acquire breasts and body hair and changes in skin texture. Some adolescents are so altered in appearance during the course of a few months that they are not recognized by people who have not seen them routinely. They hardly recognize themselves.

A body that worked smoothly in motion, that responded instantly to the demands of games, that aroused no attention at all for the most part during childhood and the juvenile and pre-adolescent phases, becomes suddenly unmanageable. It is not only subject to strange impulses and responses, its coordination is unhinged. Arms and legs are too long, voices are uncontrollable. Walking through a room becomes a veritable obstacle race, sitting down and getting up present difficulties, things in the way get broken. Adolescence is indeed "the awkward age." The awkwardness makes adolescents feel socially incompetent, the strangeness makes them uncertain about their acceptability to others, both evoke anxiety. Part of the strain of adolescence stems from these things and adolescents do not escape them until they have clearly identified what has happened to them, coordinated new resources with old and mastered new functions well enough so that their bodies operate automatically enough to be comfortably ignored once again. This takes time.

One of the conspicuous traits of adolescents is their absorption with their bodies, not merely with its sexual functions. They are as inquisitive in this respect as infants and children. They look intensely at themselves and one another, they feel and poke, they preen and adorn. Because of their conceptual resources, adolescents are more given to voyeurism and exhibitionism than children are. Like children, adolescents have a need to explore their physiological resources and discover what they can do. Unlike children, under the impulse of lust, adolescents are impelled to investigate the differences between the sexes as well as the potentialities of their own. They must also become biologically concerned with attracting the attention of the opposite sex, however deeply this is overlaid with social and cultural devices. The impulse to mate is strong in all but extremely enculturated or defective adolescents. The impulse to marry is not. Part of the struggle not infrequently observed between adolescents and their family elders in particular is the need, from the social point of view, to transform the biological need for the one into a social desire for the other.

Sensual satisfactions associated with erogenous zones of the body previous to adolescence are not associated with compelling sensations of lust directed toward others, or impulses toward reproduction. They are essentially egocentric; they most often do not involve other people at all, except, perhaps, as spectators, and when they do the people are simply instrumental means to egocentric satisfactions. The choice of person is not important. Furthermore, the erotic gratifications experienced previous to adolescence, detached from the possibility of pregnancy, involve no responsibility of a personal kind. They provide immediate pleasure while they entail neither past nor future commitments. Initially, members of the opposite sex are also viewed by adolescents as little more than mere sexual objects. The survival and cultivation of new generations and the ordering of relationships between men and women in a society require more than this. Therefore, social maturity depends upon the extension of the recognition of the intrinsic worth of others that is usually first extended to individuals of the same sex in pre-adolescence, to members of the opposite sex, so that sexual pairs can take on the attributes of friendships and be stabilized. The gratification in giving satisfaction that develops in experience with friends is an essential guarantee for the well-being of any progeny that results from these unions. This establishment of dependable and durable sexual relationships is one of the tasks of adolescence.

If the earlier phases of development have been achieved by adolescents, they begin this phase with highly developed conceptual and linguistic skills. Yet adolescents are not noted for their reasonableness or their clarity of communication. There is a good deal of extremely idiosyncratic conceptualization in the mental processes of adolescents, coupled with extensive autistic language performance. There are a number of factors that account for this.

In the first place, it takes time to conceptualize the nature of new resources, to formulate new experience, and to acquire a validated vocabulary with which to talk about them. In the second, adolescents are bound to have a set of concepts about sex and sexual behavior conveyed to them much earlier in their lives by adults, having little connection, if any, with the facts of life. These interfere with the useful conceptual differentiation of the physiological and social events of adolescence. In the third place, adolescents have been given a magical vocabulary with which to communicate about sexual matters and this, combined with their own autistic references to this subject, make for poor communication with others.

Adolescents are almost as much in the dark about what most concerns them as children are about what is happening to them, but they are better equipped to discover what they want to know. Still, this cannot be achieved immediately, and, like juveniles, adolescents need extensive communication with their peers to verify their new experience and validate their formulations about it and the vocabulary with which they talk about it. This need makes adolescents almost as dependent upon peer groups as juveniles are, though for different services. Adolescent peers are absorbed in sex and high thinking rather than games and the codes and regulations they require. The teammates of juveniles are replaced with roommates by adolescents. Nevertheless, like juveniles, adolescents are absorbed by new individual needs that make them highly egocentric. Like juveniles, adolescents need the cooperation of others to satisfy their new needs and those who do are greatly valued so long as they make their contributions. But adolescents are no more tolerant of difference than are juveniles. Those who flock together dress alike, act alike, think alike, and feel alike. Their encounters with people who are not in accord and agreement with them are frequently stormy. This often includes their elders.

One important source of the characteristic conceptual and linguistic flights of adolescents is the new conceptual ability that typically marks the onset of adolescence. In pre-adolescence, the capacity for abstract thought is initiated, with some specific social consequences. But this beginning does not characteristically lead to systematic speculation in pre-adolescents. The abstract thought of pre-adolescents is largely absorbed in the tasks of finer discriminations of perception and experience that were previously beyond their ability to know. This has been achieved by the time the fortunate young enter adolescence. On this foundation, and probably with a final addition of some psychobiologically given potential released through growth, adolescents are able to string abstractions into extensive and systematic and often intricate conceptual chains.

The appearance of an ability is almost always accompanied by its profligate use. The exercise of ability is apparently itself a source of pleasure. Babies babble as soon as they can utter distinctive sounds, children run and skip for hours as soon as they are able, juveniles ride bicycles and play games until they all but drop from fatigue and until they have perfected their skills and assured themselves that access to the means to use them will be available on call. This tendency toward obsessive use of new abilities is, perhaps, a built-in device for their development. Practice makes perfect. In any case, in the same way that the naming of things is a game for children and juveniles, the spinning of conceptual systems is a game for adolescents. Games are, by definition, activities that are not directed to necessary or practical ends. They are not means to food, clothing, or shelter. They have their own rules that are not an intrinsic part of the customs and laws that regulate routine, collective life. They do not have to take into account the conditions and necessities and pursuits of the "bread and butter" aspects of human life, either individual or collective. The conceptual systems of adolescents are no exception. Consequently, they are likely to lead adolescents who attempt to enact them into social dead ends or disaster and to exasperate those among their elders who fail to take into account that thought can be logical without being empirically sound. The application of this ability to create abstract conceptual systems to understanding, ordering, and regulating empirical social life, including their own, is one of the possible accomplishments of the adolescent phase of social development.

Jean Piaget has described this aspect of adolescence with exceptional insight and precision.[1]

> By comparison with a child, (and juvenile and pre-adolescent)[2] an adolescent is an individual who constructs systems and "theories." The child does not build systems. Those which he possesses are unconscious or preconscious in the sense that they are unformulable or unformulated so that only an external observer can understand them, while he himself never "reflects" on them. In other words, he thinks concretely, he deals with each problem in isolation and does not integrate his solutions by means of any general theories from which he could abstract a common principle. By contrast, what is striking in the adolescent is his interest in theoretical problems not yet related to everyday realities. He is frequently occupied with disarmingly naive and chimeric ideas concerning the future of the world. What is particularly surprising is his faculty for elaborating ab-

[1] Jean Piaget, *Six Psychological Studies* (New York: Random House, 1967), pp. 61-64.

[2] Piaget uses the word child to cover these three phases.

stract theories. ... The eruption of this new kind of thinking, in the form of general ideas and abstract constructions, is actually much less sudden than it would seem. It develops in relatively continuous fashion from the concrete thinking of middle childhood. (Juvenile and pre-adolescent.) The turning point occurs at about the age of twelve, after which there is rapid progress in the direction of free reflection no longer directly attached to external reality. At eleven or twelve years of age there is a fundamental transformation in the child's thinking which marks the completion of the operations constructed during middle childhood. This is the transition from concrete to "formal" thinking, or in a barbarous but clear term, "hypothetico-deductive" thinking.

Up to this age, the operations of intelligence are solely "concrete," that is, they are concerned only with reality itself and, in particular, with tangible objects that can be manipulated and subjected to real action. ... Only after the inception of formal thought, at around the age of eleven or twelve, can the mental systems that characterized adolescence be constructed. Formal operations provide thinking with entirely new ability that detaches and liberates thinking from concrete reality and permits it to build its own reflections and theories. With the advent of formal intelligence, thinking takes wings, and it is not surprising that at first this unexpected power is both used and abused. The free activity of spontaneous reflection is one of the two innovations that distinguish adolescence from childhood. (Juvenile and pre-adolescence.)

The egocentricity of adolescence is comparable to the egocentricity of the infant who assimilates the universe into his own nascent thought (symbolic play, etc.). Adolescent egocentricity is manifested by belief in the omnipotence of reflection, as though the world would submit itself to idealistic schemes rather than to systems of reality. It is the metaphysical age par excellence; ...

With so much psychobiological change in adolescents, it is not surprising that their social relationships change dramatically as well.

The interpersonal relationship of overwhelming importance to adolescents is that with the opposite sex. They have long since discovered the difference between male and female, and acquired a repertoire of manners, mores, values, rituals, formulated opinions, and what not, that are related to the fact that human beings are sexually differentiated.

But even for adolescents who grow up in societies where cultural prescriptions about maleness and femaleness extensively regulate their social cultivation and their associations from birth, the importance of members of the opposite sex that is stimulated by sexual impulses toward them is new, different, and compelling. Most adolescents view them as little more than potential sexual objects, although this fact is very frequently obscured by elaborate ideal rationalizations, many of which are in the standard cultural repertoire. As has been noted, sheer biological impulse is always egocentric. The need that rivets the attention of adolescents on the opposite sex has not been subject to the repetitive social limitations and enculturation of early training. It is extremely compelling. Therefore, even those adolescents who had begun to move away from the egocentricity of childhood and the juvenile phase during pre-adolescence revert to egocentrism in this respect. "All's fair in love" is more accurately stated as "all's fair in pursuit of sexual satisfaction."

The essential goal of adolescent relationships between the sexes is mating and it is this and its potential productive consequences that their elders are eager to prevent until the choices that adolescents make are more open to their social and cultural evaluations and their circumstance such that family units can be supported. When this obtains, adolescents themselves are inclined to seek marriage, a social and cultural phenomenon, not a biological one.

The great alteration in the exchanges between adolescents of different sexes is almost matched by that in all their other relationships. Friendships between adolescents of the same sex are often strained by the intrusion of competition between them for members of the opposite sex. At the same time, even adolescents who had begun to be less dependent on juvenile-type peer-groups and to move in more diversified pairings, are once again drawn to peer-groups of adolescents which, because of their egocentricity, are not very different from juvenile peer-groups except in the goals for which they are organized.

Finally, the relations between adolescents and their significant elders are put under great strain, not only because their interference with access to what their adolescents want is clearly evident, but because their adolescents begin to experience them as persons. The progress in conceptual differentiation of relations and connections between people, things, and events that begins in pre-adolescence includes the direction of attention to parents and other significant adults whose instrumental value had long been taken for granted. The life of adults with one another and their activities that lead to the daily provisioning of their young, are essentially unknown to children and juveniles. Pre-adolescents may begin to grasp that more has been going on than has met their eyes. Adolescents continue gathering evidence.

Initially, the discovery that parents and other adults are also people is more apt to be disconcerting than not. The fact that these are now clearly not what they had thought they were is experienced as a kind of betrayal by adolescents. Since the young do not immediately grasp the fact that their own limitations were largely the cause of past distortion, and because their thought processes are largely undisciplined and so lead them to jump to conclusions far in advance of their acquisition of adequate data to test them, they tend to assume that they have been deliberately deceived, that their parents and others have been tricking them. Once attention is drawn to the numerous discrepancies between what adults have been saying and what they have been doing, the evidence is held against them.

In the absence of knowledge of the range and complexities involved, adolescents take an all or nothing view of the social scene. The subtleties of social conventions that demand that adults speak less than the truth on many occasions, the fact that few adults are so socially mature and culturally competent that they meet the standards for performance that they espouse and demand from their young in all spheres of life or on all occasions, the fact that collective life requires more compromise than determined defense of principles, and much more, are unknown to adolescents.

A particularly indigestible fact for many adolescents is the sexual activity of adults, especially of parents. Since parents obstruct access to their own satisfactions and counsel all kinds of restraint for them, disclosure of the sexual exploits of their seniors is especially galling to the young. Besides, it is embarrassing, a derivative of anxiety. Few adolescents can imagine that the delights they are newly experiencing with each other and which they assume are unique, are attainable by their elders. Sexual play and gratification are to them unsuitable for old people, and for adolescents anyone five years older than they appears elderly, and beyond that everyone is old.

One does not need the Oedipal theory of Freud, whether this is valid or not, to account for adolescent resentment about the sexuality of their significant elders. In my opinion, heterosexual impulse in any literal sense of the term begins with the onset of adolescence, not in childhood. The conceptual abilities of adolescents are more than sufficient for them to recognize that what is new to them has been part of their elders' lives all along. In societies in which adults direct a great deal of anxiety-provoking attention to the repression of their young, a condition that obtains in most societies and is conspicuous in Western European ones, the discovery of their sexual behavior, which is in such contrast to their words, is more than enough to suggest duplicity on their part to their adolescents and to arouse both their anxiety and animosity.

The little knowledge of the adult condition and of adult life that is characteristic of adolescents is, as the proverb says, dangerous. It undermines the trust that has buttressed the relations between the young and their elders. It precipitates a series of reevaluations by adolescents of the cultural norms and prescriptions their elders have imposed on them. Much that was assumed to be given and immutable is questioned and discovered to be arbitrary. Since, in the light of the half-knowledge of adolescents, their elders appear to have lied much oftener than not and to have flouted their own commandments concerning proper behavior, they can no longer be accepted as authorities.

To believe that the people one has trusted are untrustworthy is vastly upsetting, especially when one is still dependent upon them for important goods and services. Adolescents are thrown into great insecurity thereby, and, consequently, suffer a great deal of anxiety. To be bereft of sources of information and assistance at a time when one acutely needs both tends to lead to panic. If adolescents no longer trust their elders and become suspicious of adults in general, to whom can they turn? Obviously, to one another. But although the peer-groups of adolescents relieve some of their anxiety by providing some social security, adolescents can only confirm what is within the grasp of most of them. They cannot provide one another with what they need to move out of the anxiety-fraught state of adolescence by cultivating their resources. Adolescents can only indulge one another.

The most common derivatives of anxiety are resentment and hostility. For adolescents, these are justified by the very cultural formulations about truth, justice, love, beauty and so forth, learned at their elders' knees. Or, disowning their own, adolescents pick up another set of abstract declarations from other elders to rationalize their hostility. The initial response of many adolescents who begin to see that the adult world is not what they had thought it was, that their elders are neither ideal beings nor simply instruments of more and less utility, and that they have much more to learn than they had suspected, is rejection of the prospect and the people who inhabit it. This is especially true for those adolescents who have missed the developments of pre-adolescence which would have prepared them for increasing intimacy with their elders. For those who successfully negotiated pre-adolescence, the discovery of new aspects of their elders is likely to evoke interest, just as similar discoveries in a friend did. For these, difference, and even disagreement, do not automatically threaten a relationship. It is mainly adolescents who bring to their physical phase the social resources of children and juveniles who are so disturbed by their new awareness of their elders that they close ranks against them, and, by extension, against all adults. Still, there is strain enough for all adolescents and their significant elders to make adolescence a difficult period for both.

Elders cannot satisfy the most compelling needs of adolescents. Only rarely will they be sought as sexual partners or respond if they are. Most socially mature adults have abandoned dreams of glory and of creating a world in which justice and virtue and beauty triumph for more realistic efforts to ameliorate particular conditions and to contribute a modest share to some enterprises and to the well-being of some particular people. This is the essence of the "generation gap" which is, like death and taxes, always with us, but which has been receiving much attention of late. In fact, the generation gap is conspicuous only for adolescents for the most part. There is a paradox in this.

Previous to adolescence, the gap between generations is immense, but it creates no "social problems." Children are not confused with elders nor can they successfully defy them. They do not have the capacities needed to maintain themselves. It is precisely because adolescents are on the verge of socially mature adulthood, precisely because the "gap" is rapidly narrowing, that the social distance between adolescents and their elders becomes a matter of concern and a source of tensions. Previous to adolescence the young pay very little attention to their elders as people. They have no idea of what the values or tastes or convictions or thoughts or memories of their parents and teachers *et al.*, are. Since they were not given to thought, they did not think about them. But adolescents begin to think and since they confuse discovery with instant total comprehension, their formulations are often far from adequate representations of reality, a fact that is no impediment to their convictions that they have uncovered truth. Since adolescent thought is inexperienced and likely to take the form of rather simple systems of absolute and abstract concepts and to proceed by rationalization rather than reasoning, adolescents have little patience with the qualifications proffered by their elders and consider the compromises essential for collective life downright wicked. Adolescents are often shocked by their introduction to their elders as people, not because these are really reprehensible, but because they are suddenly revealed as complex human beings.

There is a kind of strain in the typically adolescent condition in modern industrial societies which is often confused with the "generation gap," but which is only indirectly related to it. In these societies, because families no longer control access to political, economic, religious and educational resources and positions, adolescents who are on the verge of moving into adult pursuits begin to need associations with strangers. Occupational training, jobs, marriage, and other important matters depend on this. Yet adolescents have not developed social skills for dealing with strangers. They are ignorant about the adult arrangements they have to confront for the first time. They are uncertain about their own acceptability. And so, they are anxious. Adolescence is the period of extreme self-consciousness, a state about as comfortable as schizophrenic panic and not unlike it. Even requests by elders to deal directly with service people whose presence and uses have long been known to them through their parent's routine associations with them, often throw adolescents into panic. Much of their procrastination in carrying out what seem to their elders to be simple assignments is due to anxiety, not to unwillingness. Salespeople, for example, often throw adolescents into utter confusion, as do deans and doctors and prospective employers.

The adolescents who are most uncomfortable tend to cling to one another to resist the need to move into the network of adult associations. They may "drop out," proclaiming all adult performances unimportant. These tend to regress to childish, and even infantile, forms of dependence and hedonism. Other adolescents may "rebel" and band together to demand a revolution that will eliminate all the adult relationships and organizations which they are finding it difficult to enter into. It is not fortuitous that so many adolescents abandon their radical beliefs and organizations as soon as they succeed in making their way into what is currently called "the establishment." Many of these improve on example and become doggedly conservative. This change takes no coercion by elders or authorities. Relief from acute anxiety and the discovery of the satisfactions afforded by the acquisition and exercise of competence are more than enough to evoke and sustain it.

Of the two most common extreme reactions by adolescents to the prospect of having to maintain themselves with the help of strangers, each of whom must be persuaded to cooperate with them, rebellion is the more likely to lead into the social maturity of early adulthood. It does not involve serious regression. The preoccupation of rebellious adolescents with systems of thought exercises their apparatus for thought, thereby potentially improving its function and their grasp of reality. The sporadic efforts of these adolescents to enact their schemes teach them something about the need for compromise in the interest of collective action. Their opposition teaches them that there are multiple responses to similar things and events and that more than one may be reasonable. Finally, some of them become aware of their ignorance and lack of skills and acquire the desire to learn. Since they can only learn what they want to know from their elders, they begin to make their peace with them. To the extent that they recognize the competence of their elders, they come to respect them.

Once these developments take place, adolescence is ending. Many young people have been fortunate enough to negotiate them without being driven to the extreme of seriously rejecting their elders and thus denying themselves whatever assistance they can provide. In societies in which families and ascribed relationships in prescribed hierarchies are the basis of organization, extreme adolescent reactions are uncommon. There is much less that is likely to evoke anxiety for adolescents in such arrangements. They do not have to cope with strangers. Their access to the associations which they begin to see as necessary for their adult maintenance is clear and assured. It is only when this is not the case, when adolescents have to fend for themselves in large measure to achieve essential interpersonal connections, that both more and less permanent social casualties and disruptive rebellion are conspicuous among adolescents. Adolescence as a stage of development is not itself a manifestation of pathology.

The cultural categories that have special relevance for adolescence are the rules and norms and values associated with sexual satisfactions and the relations of males and females, especially in marriage. Everywhere, adolescent males are prepared for adult occupations. Adolescence is assumed to be the last step to maturity. Biologically, it is; socially, it may or may not be. In any case, adolescent males are viewed as new recruits to man the elaborate network of organizations and perform the tasks that constitute societies. Furthermore, in most societies, adolescence is the last period in which the young can expect total support from their elders and occupational training is designed to equip them to maintain themselves. Training in domestic skills has been required of female adolescents until recent times. This has changed somewhat in highly industrialized societies. In these, most females do not escape the need to acquire them, but they are more likely to pick them up in in-service training after marriage. Still, most female adolescents are still expected to become proficient in domestic management and housekeeping. Other occupational training is optional, even in technologically advanced societies.

Adolescents continue to be subject to all the coercions that have been exercised by adults and their peers before. Some of them, in modern societies, and especially in urban areas, begin to experience the restraints of law: the deliberately enacted regulations of localities and societies. Until this time, most young people are shielded from direct experience with law by their elders. But as adolescents, they begin to be required to have licenses for working, for driving, for owning a dog, for fishing, for marrying, and so forth. If they earn money, they can be subject to taxation. If military arrangements require it, they become subject to military draft. In some traditional societies, adolescence itself confers full membership and adolescents become responsible to the full range of customary authority in their societies. In short, the obligations of citizenship begin to impinge on adolescents.

Since these often demand great limitation on individual action and command some particular performances and the contribution of material wealth, they are not likely to evoke voluntary compliance from many members of a population, certainly not from adolescents whose understanding of their contribution to social order and services, and hence indirectly to individuals, is sketchy, if it exists at all. Therefore, experience of law is correlated with police powers of coercion. Since even children come to accept what cannot be avoided with voluntary compliance, however grudging, and juveniles are ardent supporters of collective order, and since most adults have at least the social competence of children and juveniles, most of them comply with the laws of their society when they encounter them, at least as long as they believe they cannot elude its enforcement agents.

So do most adolescents, and for the same reason. But to those adolescents for whom elders are conceived as betrayers and hypocrites, general laws are equated with all the other "exploitive" demands of "phony" adults. Having concluded that their particular elders conspired against them, they conclude that another set, usually labeled "the government" or "the establishment," or "society," or "they," is involved in a self-serving conspiracy at the expense of the whole population, or, even of mankind.

Their penchant for spinning conceptual schemes, or espousing those of others, is used to validate this conviction, and validation is confused by them with verification. This category of adolescent is very apt to respond to the spate of new restrictions and demands made upon them as budding citizens, and to the agents of enforcement, with all the powers of resistance at their command, including force, which, for some of them, is a manifestation of social regression. There are essentially only three major factors that move such adolescents from defiance to compliance. The first is the application of external force greater than their own, which is the first and the ultimate form of coercion that limits individual impulse in the interest of collective requirements. The second is their voluntary subordination to a particular person who, for any number of possible reasons, is considered the exception that proves to them that all other people in authority are evil and who, therefore, becomes invested with all authority for them, so to speak. The third, and most useful in the long run to them and to their fellow citizens, is the application of their mental abilities to the understanding of the world they live in, in contrast to the construction of utopias.

Adolescents are also coerced by their own compelling need to establish relatively durable relations with the opposite sex. Nothing so readily induces adolescents to meet the current cultural prescriptions for sexual attractiveness as his or her interest in a particular girl or boy. If cleanliness is indicated, bathing becomes an obsession for adolescents whose parents had not succeeded in getting them to wash their hands for meals without a daily struggle. If thinness defines sexual beauty, fat boys and girls become slim adolescents at whatever cost in oral gratifications. If physical prowess is the sexual fashion, it is achieved; if a passion for or against particular interests and activities, it is displayed; if stupidity in females, it is feigned. What no amount of adult coercion could have achieved appears almost as if by magic when adolescents are in pursuit of mates. This is a powerful incentive for the acquisition of new cultural modifications.

All forms of interaction are within the competence of adolescents who have negotiated the preceding stages of development. For these, from adolescence onward, the forms-of-interaction that characterize particular exchanges between people will depend largely on cultural definitions of what is socially appropriate. In traditional China, for example, the young were always subordinate to the old, and men were always superordinate in their relations to women, except to their mothers. However, adolescents are highly competitive with one another in pursuit of mates unless the conventions of their society decree that these are chosen by their elders. Otherwise, they are very cooperative with one another.

The shift in their relations with adults, expecially their significant elders, is rarely smooth unless the conventions define this as a subordinate relationship for life. Otherwise, it is the problem of adolescents to move from dependency and subordination toward equality with their elders. Effective achievement of this goal requires their acquisition of the knowledge and skills of their elders, and this takes years. In the meantime, adolescents are inclined to assert an equality that does not exist in fact. The realities of existence often force them to retreat from this assertion. They are still dependent in important respects.

Uncertainties in the progress to a stable relationship on a new level of interaction with elders make for anxiety, especially if the elders with whom the adolescents deal are also uncertain about what is happening and where it leads. And so the relations between adolescents and their elders oscillate from something close to the superordinate-subordinate patterns of infancy and childhood in which first one and then the other dominates, through the kind of adaptive cooperation of juveniles that is effective for many kinds of activity, to the possibility of collaboration based on mutual knowledge of what their elders are as individuals and conviction of their intrinsic worth. This can be achieved in adolescence, and when it is adolescents are on the threshold of social adulthood.

Full realization of the potentialities of adolescence which lead to domestic and occupational competence is obviously a vital step toward individual biological and social maturity. From a biological point of view, no organism has reached maturity until it can and does reproduce itself. This is a species requirement for survival. Adolescence is also the last phase in which significant new physical resources are made available. The initial stages of development are periods of exceptional growth because they modify pre-existing states and break up earlier adaptations and techniques for living and thus provide rich opportunity for change and addition. This is one reason why they are likely to be unstable periods, and risky. It is possible to lose previously established means to satisfactions and maintenance that worked without acquiring effective new ones. Adolescence is a particularly vulnerable phase, but it is often the last opportunity for major personal development.

Socially, stable sexual unions and family groups are essential to insure the maintenance of populations, social organizations, and the transmission of cultural accumulations that are necessary for human life in general. This involves more than mere physiological accomplishments. Competent performance of the functions of parenthood requires considerable social maturity in the parents. Childish parents are a disaster for children. Competent performance also requires extensive familiarity with the culture that the young will need in their particular social settings. Irrelevant enculturation has been a handicap to the children of immigrants more often than inadequate capacity for human relationships.

Finally, the maintenance and expansion of cultural accumulations that are the chief means for human development, both individual and collective, require the cultivation of the adolescent resources for thought. It is the abstract thinking of human beings that has enabled them to increase continuously both their control over their environment and their expansion of it. The realm of complex social phenomena depends on it.

Clearly, much that is significant for the social maturity of individuals and for collective human life depends upon the achievement of the developments that become possible in adolescence. Once these are acquired, individuals move into a new phase of social development. They become young adults and, if their social environment has been fortunate, they join the ranks of the socially mature. But the period of social development called adolescence is obviously difficult, and a good many people, wherever they live, do not master its resources. Socially adolescent, but chronologically adult, individuals are numerous in adult populations.

The continuation of adolescent sexual behavior into later life is rather a nuisance. Failure to stabilize their sexual impulses keeps aging adolescents in continuous pursuit of this goal. These are the Don Juans and perpetually flirtatious women who view all members of the opposite sex as little more than objects of potential physical satisfaction, who project an ideal-typical romantic character on each one who attracts them, but who find every actual encounter disappointing. Their rationalization for their inability to establish durable relationships with a member of the opposite sex is usually the pursuit of the ideal. Like young adolescents they remain irresponsible toward particular others and, therefore, are grossly inadequate spouses and parents.

Another kind of fatality that is a common result of adolescent experience is failure to view the opposite sex as a sexual object at all. The possible impediments to the development of heterosexual relationships are many, but they add up to an impenetrable barrier of anxiety that is evoked by impulses toward this eventuality. The sources of this anxiety can be many, but some of them are often found in overcomplexity of the conditions that surround adolescent experience. Since sexual impulses are universal and compelling, other means for releasing sexual tension are found. Homo-erotic relationships are one solution. If the individuals who seek this solution have developed the resources of pre-adolescence, their relationships are often stable and satisfying. if not, they are likely to persist only so long as they are immediately gratifying. In societies in which homo-erotic exchanges are culturally proscribed, these prohibitions and threats of punishment themselves tend to interfere with comfortable adaptations of this kind. The childish among these people are highly exploitive.

Finally, in the absence of heterosexual adaptations, or even homosexual ones, the variety of erotic gratifications that characterize manipulations of erogenous zones of the body from infancy onward may become the chief, if not the sole, means to sexual satisfaction. Insofar as social maturity entails parenthood, either a homosexual solution to sexual impulse or any of the numerous other chiefly autoerotic satisfactions are an impediment to achieving it.

The social impact of adolescents of any age is succinctly described by Jean Piaget:

> Exactly parallel to the elaboration of the formal operations and the completion of the constructions of thought, adolescent affectivity asserts itself through the development of the personality and its injection into adult society. . . . The young child unwittingly models the world in his own image but nonetheless feels inferior to adults and the older children whom he imitates. He thus fashions a kind of separate world at a level below the world of his elders. The adolescent, on the other hand, . . . sees himself as equal to his elders, yet different from them, different because of the new life stirring in him. He wants to surpass and astound them by transforming the world. That is why the adolescent's system or life plans are at the same time filled with generous sentiments and altruistic or mystically fervent projects and with disquieting megalomania and conscious egocentricity. . . .
>
> The synthesis of these projects of social cooperation and self-evaluation signals the disequilibrium of the nascent personality and often appears as a form of Messianism. The adolescent in all modesty attributes to himself an essential role in the salvation of humanity and organizes his life plans accordingly. . . .
>
> We see, then, how the adolescent goes about injecting himself into adult society. He does so by means of projects, life plans, theoretical systems, and ideas of political or social reform. In short, he does so by means of thinking and almost, one might say, by imagination—so far does his hypothetico-deductive thinking sometimes depart from reality.
>
> The society that interests him is the society he wants to reform; he has nothing but disdain or disinterest for the real

society he condemns. Furthermore, adolescent sociability develops through the young person's interactions with other adolescents. It is highly instructive to compare the social interaction of adolescents with that of children. The latter association has as its essential goal the collective game or, less frequently, . . . concrete common work. Adolescent interaction, on the other hand, is aimed primarily at discussion. Whether in twosomes or in small coteries, the world is reconstructed in common, and the adolescent loses himself in endless discussion as a means of combating the real world. Sometimes there is mutual criticism of respective solutions, but there is general agreement as to the absolute necessity for reform. Then come broader interactions and young people's movements, where attempts at positive reorganization are made and great collective enthusiasms are exhibited.[3]

Whether or not the continuation of the characteristic mental and affective activities of adolescence into adult life is constructive or destructive for collective living depends upon the nature of the messianic or idealistic schemes of the socially adolescent adults. Startling discovery and invention are not apt to be made by individuals who are firmly attached to empirical realities. The adult realm has need of some dreamers. It needs some votaries for ideals which the socially mature well understand are not capable of realization, but which serve them as symbols of direction for more mundane strivings.

The "metaphysical" nature of adolescent thought and the affect that accompanies it are well suited to this. Very great artists, scientists, explorers, and religious and political reformers have been remarkably naive about the ways of the world and have often been sexually childish or adolescent as well. Many have been appallingly irresponsible toward particular other people with whom they lived while espousing the well-being and contributing to the glories of mankind. Perusal of the lives of saints reveals a distressing taste for destroying heretics and remarkable insensitivity to the needs of their near and dear. Nevertheless, few would wish that these people had led more responsible lives in the interest of domestic and civil felicity.

[3] Piaget, *Six Psychological Studies*, pp. 64-69.

However, not all adult adolescents are gifted, and the "ideals" that many espouse are more childish than concern with human salvation or the improvement of the world. Physical adolescence impinges on everyone, whatever their levels of social skill. The combination of a child's egocentrism and conception of others as mere instruments in its service with unstable adolescent strivings and physical maturity is socially undesirable. People of this type are both cynical and naive. They are also exploitive. Their services can be bought for any purpose so long as it serves their own ends. They will, as the saying goes, betray their own grandmothers if that will bring them even small immediate advantages. They are often glib speakers and clever rationalizers. They may even be exceptionally skilled in some ways. But, if social maturity is defined as the transformation of individuals into dependable social units in relationships and complex associations, adult adolescents of this type fall far short of it. They are among the more destructive elements in adult collective life.

However, despite the hazards of adolescence, for those who have succeeded in negotiating the earlier stages of social development, it is a period of great potential improvement. Fortunate adolescents are usually eager to take the next important steps toward the relative autonomy of adult life. Many move into adult involvements with considerable ease. The end of tutelage in parental homes and in schools and the initiation of their own households and self-sustaining occupations and careers are experienced as a stimulating expansion of personal competence, satisfactions, and freedom. Strangers come to be experienced as socially neutral. Particular other people, rather than categories of them, such as the poor, the sick, and the oppressed, are once again endowed with intrinsic importance. Hopefully, this gift is extended to elders and members of the opposite sex. In any case, once marital and occupational choices are made, and some competence for both is achieved, adolescents enter the ranks of mature young adults.

Chapter Seven

Social Maturity

ALTHOUGH THE UPPER LIMITS of social maturity are open-ended and what is considered adult competence is determined in particular instances by the social and cultural characteristics of particular societies, its threshold is discernible. When the adaptation of the young to other people finally establishes some of them as equivalent in significance to themselves and includes their general and constant responsibility to the people among whom they live, they have moved out of adolescence. When their capacity for conceptual thought includes verified representations of empirical experience, thereby curtailing the "metaphysics" and "megalomania" of adolescence, young adults manifest the "grasp of reality" associated with social maturity that enables them to expand their abilities and cope with the demands that responsibility for others imposes.

No healthy organism voluntarily gives up the pursuit of the satisfaction of its needs, and humans are no exception. But socially mature young adults have evolved a repertoire of culturally defined interpersonal needs that limit and, on occasion, supplant organic needs. Gratification in giving satisfaction to others becomes a powerful motive in socially mature individuals that greatly enhances their reliability in relations with others and as participants in collective enterprises.

One conspicuous indication that young adults have crossed the threshold of maturity is the bridging of the social gap between themselves and elders. The conceptual grasp of reality that includes an expanding awareness of the human condition in general and of that of some others in particular finally transforms the members of the generation that tended and supplied and coerced and cultivated the young into fully human people of varying degrees of interest to them. Once social maturity is reached, difference in age rapidly ceases to be a barrier to relationships of intimacy, or even of equality.

After social maturity is achieved, subsequent development involves the expansion of resources more than their inception, the maintenance of personal integration rather than its achievement. However, although social maturity involves the domination of sheer biological states and impulses by conceptual interference, i.e., self-regulation, the socially mature are not freed from the demands of their bodies. Adaptation to and subordination of somatic change are almost as conspicuous at the end of the life cycle as they are at its beginning. Both are marked by biological events that are beyond the control of the individuals who undergo them. The maintenance of social maturity depends as much upon how well or badly they adapt to inevitable physical changes and their interpersonal consequences as earlier phases of social development do and so this period can usefully be subdivided into young adulthood, middle age, and old age.

Young Adulthood

Young adults begin to be responsible for the maintenance of both the biological and social aspects of collective human life. Previous to this stage of social development, individuals are essentially on the receiving end of the production of goods and services and of social and cultural cultivation in all societies. Once they reach social maturity, they enter the ranks of the people who maintain, produce, and transmit all the ingredients necessary for the perpetuation of human life, including the social factors and conditions which distinguish it from all other forms of life and on which its survival depends. This is an extremely demanding phase of existence for individuals, but, since it includes a great deal of new personal development, it is experienced by those who master it with great satisfaction. The expansion of personal competence is a solid contribution to the self-esteem of everyone. The major areas of expansion for young adults are domestic and occupational. Marriage, parenthood, and the activities that support them define the horizons of the majority in this category.

Biologically, early adulthood is marked by full somatic growth. Nothing more in the way of individual psychobiological resources can be expected to be made available as a result of mere growth. Potentially, this is the period of greatest skill in physical activities. Presumably, these individuals have escaped "growing pains" and are not yet subject to the "aches and pains" that are the result of inevitable degenerative processes. Therefore, optimally, all the activities important to societies that require physical stamina and skill are for the most part undertaken by young adults: childbearing, military service, exploration, construction, sports, some of the performing arts, and so forth.

This is not usually the period of greatest mental and linguistic competence. As we have noted, the somatic resources needed for these do not mature until relatively late in the life-cycle. Their development requires complex social conditions and considerable effort over time. Furthermore, in the absence of physical deterioration that involves the central nervous system, mental and linguistic capacities can be expanded to the end of life.

However, early social maturity is characterized by the application of the capacity for evolving systems of thought to the understanding, development, and regulation of the realities of direct experience. The spinning of metaphysical webs of thought that is so typical for adolescents, ceases to be of great interest to socially mature adults, unless they have made this a profession. Capacity for logical progressions of thought, for analysis and synthesis, for the expansion of knowledge by the use of analogy, the identification of classes of phenomena, for reasoning, etc. is an attribute of early human maturity. This is what is meant by what Harry Stack Sullivan called the "syntaxic mode of conceptualization." It makes possible the rational inference and deduction that greatly elaborates and expands direct experience.

This return to concrete reality combined with capacity for abstract thought adds a new dimension to the scope of attention of mature young adults. From this time onward, foresight, the formulation of probable events in the relatively near future, increasingly determines current decisions and activities. Foresight should not be confused with the daydreaming of children or the total and absolute schemes for reforming the world projected to eternity that absorb adolescents. Foresight depends upon hindsight, the formulation of experience that is recorded in the mysterious processes we call memory and is, therefore, subject to relatively easy recall into awareness. Foresight represents a marked increase in human adaptation to other people and the conditions for the maintenance of human life that greatly enhances the ability of individuals to achieve satisfactions and security for themselves and the particular others for whom they are responsible while they indirectly, and usually inadvertently, maintain their societies and culture as well.

The manifestation of foresight is one of the clearest indications that an adolescent has moved into the sphere of the socially mature. Nothing enrages an adolescent more than the restricting qualifications to his dreams that the foresight of his elders compels them to bring to his attention. Psychiatric disclosures suggest that the nearer he is to mature recognition of the mundane facts of life, the more violent his resistance to these suggestions. This seems to be a kind of last fling of unfettered imagination before the acceptance of the fact that man is an earth creature. For idealistic adolescents, as for Don Quixote, the "impossible dream" is all and if its pursuit ends in disaster, this is taken as proof for the need to change the world so that the human spirit can triumph, not as a spur to modification of their own performances. These flights are indeed a triumph of the human ability to think abstractly, but this remarkable and uniquely human capacity can endanger both individual and collective survival. Human maturity requires the ability to recognize a windmill for what it is and to act accordingly.

Highly individual, non-validated, and even pre-conceptual elements persist in the mental operations of everyone. Except for those that occur in sleep, they are mostly maladaptive intrusions and if an individual continues to use too many of them he is in trouble. No human being is completely rational. It would not serve him well if he could achieve this because it would too grossly interfere with some basic somatic functions.[1] But it is a mark of human maturity to be able to think logically when necessary. People do not think as often as they believe they do. The word is used more magically than not. However, when something interrupts habitual or automatic responses, or changed conditions demand new ones, socially mature human beings take to thought as their means for resolving their difficulties.

What is true for the mental processes of the socially mature is true for their linguistic ones as well. The two are closely interconnected, though how and in what ways are little understood as yet. The continuously expanding range of verbal communication that is part of everyone's experience as he grows up gradually refines speech and attaches it to an accumulation of consensually validated meanings. The meanings are primarily based on prevailing cultural definitions and on experience that is widely shared by a population. Meaning is a social phenomenon. By the time individuals reach early maturity, their language performances have become fairly precise. They use language as a tool for formulating their experience and thoughts and for communicating them to the people among whom they live. For the most part, the magical use of words has been recognized as a child's game. Obviously, no one's linguistic abilities are so perfectly evolved that all autistic elements are excluded, but most autistic usages are dropped because they have come to be seen as impediments to communication and cooperative action.

In literate societies, the acquisition of skill in a written language is a necessary part of social maturity. One way of keeping a category of people in these societies subjugated to another category is to prevent their achievement of social competence by keeping them illiterate. In societies in which social organization depends upon complex technological skills, illiteracy is a crippling social handicap. As the complexity of technology increases, and with it the com-

[1] This is interestingly discussed in A. T. W. Simeons, M.D., *Man's Presumptuous Brain* (New York: E. P. Dutton, 1962).

plexity of social organization, the level of development of both mental skills and oral and written linguistic ability required for adult competence is raised. This is one of the factors that makes the achievement of social maturity more hazardous in complex industrial societies than it is in tribal communities or traditional societies. It also raises the age at which it is likely to be manifest. This is apparent in the extension of the time spent in formal education in these societies and in the fact that in an increasing number of occupations, the competence required even for initial participation keeps more and more people in training until they are in their late twenties.

It is clear that one of the innovations of modern human life is this increased dependence upon the cultivation of human mental and linguistic abilities, not only of the range of mental skills themselves, but of their distribution in populations. It is difficult to determine whether or not the manifestations of human mental capacity are being augmented, but there is no doubt that these skills are being cultivated in more and more people. If biological evolution is correlated with natural selection based on efficient adaptation in the long run to the demands made upon organisms, it seems that adult maturity in general for human beings will include even more highly developed mental skills than it does at present. Even now, a high degree of self-regulation that depends upon the superordination of conceptual organization of experience over somatic impulse is an essential trait of the socially mature adult in complex, heterogeneous, industrial societies.

The interpersonal relationships of young adults are conspicuously different from those of adolescents. From birth to early adulthood, individuals everywhere live within a circle of associations of which their home is the center. In complex societies they move from it to schools, churches, play and peer-groups, and so forth, but from each of these they return home. Even the selection of the particular non-family groups in which they participate is largely determined by their "home circle." Parents and parent surrogates are the source of support and overall cultivation and guidance. In tribal communities, basic spheres of living —familial, economic, political, religious, educational, recreational, etc.—tend to be organized in a set of concentric circles. The basic social influences, demands, and opportunities are much the same for everyone and family relations dominate them throughout the life-cycle.

In more complex societies, family control is exercised chiefly for the young from a center that is related to other essential areas as the hub of a wheel is to its spokes and perimeter. Families and other organizations do not penetrate one another, they impinge with respect to some of their functions only. Families have considerable power to determine which spokes their particular young will follow to the perimeter, but they do not control the functions represented by the spokes in this analogy and the nearer that their young get to the perimeter the smaller their influence over them. Once the young reach the perimeter, if they are able to maintain themselves, they need not return to the hub. When this happens, as it does for the majority in complex societies, the social circle determined by families for the most part no longer encompasses the social life of the young. They become relatively autonomous, a characteristic of social maturity.

In modern societies in which the social range of adult relationships is open-ended, the maintenance of individuals as well as of the society depends upon cooperation between strangers many of whom are conspicuously different from one another in such important respects as education, religion, race, ethnic traits, and political beliefs. All such difference tends to evoke anxiety and defenses against it in individuals unless they have been trained to deal with it. Therefore, the social ability to deal with strangers and social and cultural heterogeneity is essential for mature adults in these societies. In a world in which isolation between populations is being eliminated by technical means of transportation and communication and the interlocking technical means of production, this social skill is becoming a requirement for social maturity everywhere.

Life in modern, highly technologically developed societies also requires the ability to act as an effective social unit in large organizations made up of a variety of strangers. The contractual nature of membership in corporations and large administrative organizations, the impersonality of the direct reciprocities between the people in them, and the anonymity of many who are, nonetheless, interdependent in important respects, requires a great deal of self-regulation on the part of the participants in them. It also requires facility in written as well as oral communication.

This kind of social development was not necessary in tribal communities or traditional societies. It lengthens the time involved in reaching adult social competence in complex societies. Children, juveniles, and pre-adolescents are too dependent on direct personal relationships and their family and peer-groups either to operate effectively in or to benefit from corporate organizations. The acquisition of this ability is one of the possible accomplishments of late adolescence and, in modern societies, it is a necessary development for social maturity in young adults.

This has numerous social consequences. It delays the achievement of ability to be self-supporting for many years and thus the attainment of a comfortable level of individual social autonomy. This influences marriage and child-rearing. An early pregnancy, because it puts an end to a wife's career as a wage-earner and increases the economic demands upon a husband, can also condemn him to a permanent limitation to his potential achievements by forcing him to abandon or curtail his professional training prematurely. The range of training and its cost increase constantly and are already beyond the means of most parents to supply. This has led to social innovations to supply tax money and government support for young adults in training. This raises the problems of government requisites for assistance. These and many other changes alter the relationships between parents and children, citizens and their governments. They have changed, and are changing political and educational and economic institutions. They are a source of strain in the early adult life of people in industrial societies. However, there are assets for them as well as liabilities.

Despite the new strains imposed by life in modern, complex societies, the range of impersonal associations which they require actually potentially increases both individual freedom and security. Dependence on a few people for many services involves great risk because the loss of one of

them disrupts access to a large number of important satisfactions and it becomes increasingly difficult to find a substitute willing to provide as much. Furthermore, this kind
of dependency restricts the possible range of satisfactions
since it cannot transcend the limits of the personal resources of a few.

Dependence on a large number of people, each of whom
supplies a very limited number of satisfactions, augments
security because they are rather easily replaced. It expands
the range of satisfactions available, because new people can
be added to supply new goods and services. The classified
telephone directory of the large cities of industrial societies
is a measure of the possibilities that can be made available
with little or no personal involvement. More goods and services can be distributed to more people.

Somewhat paradoxically, although young adults in
modern societies must develop abilities for cooperation
with strangers in impersonal associations to a high degree, it
is responsibility to the needs of particular others that is,
perhaps, the essential quality that marks the beginning of
social maturity. It takes root in pre-adolescence, but the
opportunities for satisfaction in giving satisfaction for
chronological pre-adolescents are relatively few. The strains
of adolescence tend to interfere with the smooth progress
of the developments of pre-adolescence by plunging adolescents into profound egocentricity again. Idealized concern
for idealized mankind, or parts thereof, does not interfere
with it; responsiveness to particular people does. When
adolescents move toward concern for the well-being of
some particular people again, one knows that they have
negotiated the transformations of adolescence successfully.

Socially mature young adults establish new family units
in which spouses view each other as far more than mere
instruments to sexual satisfaction or physical maintenance.
As parents, they take pleasure in giving satisfaction to their
young children, who can hardly provide many other satisfactions. As sons and daughters to aging parents, recognition of services rendered them in the past makes whatever
attention their parents may need from them a means to
express their newly discovered appreciation. Mature young
adults are dependable colleagues, co-workers, employees,

customers, and suppliers. In short, in social terms, they become humane.

The cultural formulations that are most significant for socially mature young adults are those concerned with family life and domestic and occupational skills. It is especially an indication of social maturity when young adults stop responding to all cultural demands that are not either unnoticed or are no hindrance to their egocentric pursuits as arbitrary intrusions to be resisted if possible. When this happens, they begin voluntarily to seek to acquire particular cultural resources and voluntarily to abide by rules and regulations in general, if not to a particular set of them, because they have come to see that cooperation and the coordination of the activities of large numbers of people are impossible without them. This much at least must characterize the socially mature.

The socially mature avoid a good deal of individual strain because they have finally come to want to do what needs to be done, and even what it took years of repetitive coercions by numerous adults to get them to do in the first place. This includes innumerable things from wanting to brush their teeth, to wanting to hold down a demanding job and to be sexually faithful in a monogamous marriage, and even to wanting to serve in the armed forces of their societies. They have acquired a new category of needs and motives which, except for the acquisition of a language, is the most important result of enculturation.

This category of "interpersonal" or "social" needs, the satisfaction of which often takes precedence over the satisfaction of somatic needs for millions of people, is solely the outcome of social and cultural modification by other people. Human biology alone would never lead to it. These needs make no biological sense at all. But collective social order, which is a biological requirement for human beings, depends upon this peculiar and peculiarly human cultivation of psychobiological resources and, once it is achieved, it is painless for individuals because it is an adjunct to the pursuit of interpersonal needs which are experienced as their own. The imposition of cultural prerequisites between felt organic need and its satisfaction as a condition for attaining satisfaction by training elders results in making the cultural requirements themselves a source of individual motivation.

This raises the question of stability and change, of how much of any existing social order is necessary and how much of what is necessary is the best available arrangement for meeting the needs of a population, as opposed to what merely happens to exist. This is not easy to ascertain. Systematic study can only be applied to what exists, or has existed. In the study of physical and biological phenomena, or of historical record, or of a category of artifacts, there is no debate as to the existence of an item under consideration or as to the boundaries that distinguish it from all other phenomena. Given the establishment of boundaries, whatever maintains them is assumed to be essential to the phenomena. But social and cultural phenomena have no such visible boundaries and even their existence is often more a matter of inference than demonstrable proof.

Therefore, it is more difficult to identify criteria for what is essential to social phenomena. Reference to their impact on human beings is unsatisfactory because this depends on a great many factors, many of which are not identifiable until long after the event, if at all. Reference to the maintenance of the phenomena is unsatisfactory because it involves a kind of iteration that something is because it is and must be what it is, which is not necessarily so for man-made phenomena. It is not surprising that social scientists are often accused of automatic support for whatever status quo they happen to deal with. Even those who focus on social processes and change are forced to identify something fixed in order to identify what changes.

Arbitrary cultural formulations determine many of the institutional arrangements in a society at any given time, but not what must be, a fact commonly referred to as "cultural relativism." However, this fact should not be taken to imply that all human arrangements are merely relative to the accidents of cultural formulation, even though some of them surely will be. Human psychobiology, the nature of organization itself, and limits imposed by the characteristics of physical and biological phenomena do set limits to what is possible for human beings and determine the better part of the routine arrangements of mankind.

The ingenuity and cultural modifiability of human beings tend to obscure these limits, but their disclosure provides a basis for defining the cultural aspects of phenomena by subtracting from them what is not cultural.

The forms of social phenomena and their cultural elaborations are far more varied than the functions they serve. To say that social order is essential for collective human life, which is itself essential for the survival, maintenance, and development of individual human beings, and to say that if social order is to be relatively stable it must be supported by the self-regulation of the majority of its adult members according to consensually validated rules, is not to say that any particular social and cultural arrangement is essential for all mankind or that it is the best for the particular people who live with it. It does say that if the social organizations and institutions of a society are to be maintained, the adults in the population must be socially mature enough to limit voluntarily their impulses for individual gratification to the extent required for their collective cooperation and pursue their individual ends within a range of means that are widely accepted.

Much of the on-going daily life of individuals is irrelevant to the maintenance of the overall social arrangements in which they live.[2] There are many areas of improvisation in which individuals are free to express themselves, to seek individuated satisfactions, to use creative powers. How much particular people can benefit from these unsupervised and undefined opportunities depends upon their own talents and their level of cultivation.

A limited version of this aspect of human living is sometimes discussed under the heading of "Leisure," defined as time in which people do as they please. There are many more moments of leisure than those officially provided on Sundays, holidays, and vacations. At the far end of a continuum of opportunities for socially unprescribed activities is the member of a board of directors doodling on his scratch pad, an actor with a twenty-minute period of silence on stage who produced a very funny book of verse

[2] Fred Katz, *Autonomy and Organization* (New York: Random House, 1968).

in the time provided, a diplomat who used the leisure available in long conferences for autobiographical recall, and the chairman of an academic department who created and solved chess problems under similar circumstances. The "coffee break" has been institutionalized, but it began as improvisation. Even such highly individual gratifications as those provided by various sexual exchanges are not infrequently achieved during office hours.

In short, the notion that the maintenance of social order absorbs all the energies of those who live in it and that the limitation of individual impulse needed to meet routine collective demands precludes individual satisfactions, is often overstated. Lester Ward, a sociologist rarely mentioned these days, summed up the actual condition of socially mature adults in their societies in a definition of virtue which, he suggested, is not rejection, but suitable choice, and the avoidance of inappropriate time and place. This virtue is primarily achieved by the progressive social development of individuals so that, as adults, they can make suitable choices and avoid inappropriate times and places in the societies in which they live. When they can, no one bothers to check on what they do on their own time.

Besides, few people are so socially and culturally modified that some impulses for immediate and exclusive gratification do not survive in them. It is possible that they all do, which is what is implied in the Freudian concept of the "id." But awareness of dependence upon others and the need for the approval of some of them for cooperation in attaining individual ends keep the threat of the earlier forms of coercion operative. However elaborate, the conditions for keeping a job are still the conditions for access to food, clothing, and shelter. The evocation of tenderness and attention from significant others continues to depend upon some measure of approval by them. Participation in collective life with peers always depends upon the maintenance of some standards if ostracism is to be avoided.

However, the self-regulation of socially mature adults eliminates the need of direct coercions of this kind. What is generally expected of individuals becomes what they expect of themselves. Self-esteem replaces the need for constant reassurance in the form of manifestations of approval by all others. The happy consequence of these developments is the great decrease in occasions for anxiety. It is in early social adulthood that people can escape life on the anxiety-gradient that is inescapable for the young and immature. This degree of freedom from anxiety itself makes way for comfortable adaptation to a greater number and variety of people and the possibility of establishing relationships of intimacy with some of them. It also enhances ability to cope with new social situations, a skill that bodes well for the next stages of life. Extreme conformity to local culture and concern for what everyone thinks are signs of excessive anxiety, not of mature enculturation.

The reduction of anxiety evoked by other people (anxiety is only evoked by other people) frees socially mature adults to respond to others in whatever form of interaction is appropriate to a relationship or social situation. It even enables them to fit their responses to their own immediate sentiments in some measure. It is up to mature adults to make "suitable choices."

Doctrinal declarations about absolute equality in terms of personal potential, skills, and competence between all people do not coincide with reality. The young cannot equal their elders and no one at any age is competent at everything. Therefore, for everyone, subordination continues to be an appropriate response to some people, either because they have some particular attribute of their own, or because they represent collective arrangements that must take precedence over individuals if they are to serve them.

Games and the pursuit of limited items by people of relative equality make competition a conspicuous form of interaction between adults in all societies that are not dominated by a hierarchy of ascribed relationships. The difference between the exercise of competition by the socially mature and competition between the immature is that the former are sufficiently self-regulated to insure that a competitive situation will not break down into one of conflict. Competition is an extremely unstable form-of-interaction among the immature. Most of the interactions between mature adults take the form of voluntary cooperation. It is a form-of-interaction that is effective between strangers as well as between intimates.

Finally, mature adults collaborate with some people. Their intrinsic value and the gratifications derived from providing their satisfactions evoke this form of interaction in which individuals come close to dealing with one another as extensions of themselves. Among mature adults, this extension is not restricted to people like themselves, as it is for the most part in the pre-adolescent phase. Conceptual development includes the ability to identify states of being and interests in others different from one's own. Some come to be shared, some do not. But collaboration expands the social choices available to each collaborator by making what is available to each of them available to the other.

This form of interaction is so much rarer than the others in human life that it is not often differentiated from co-operation. The immature cannot recognize it. It has been most clearly revealed, perhaps, in the limited instances of collaboration that sometimes occur between scholars, or scientists, or explorers, for example. They may even be incapable of collaboration in any area of living other than that of their major interest, but they have been known to exercise it to a high degree in particular circumstances. In these cases, all the knowledge and skill which anyone possesses are made available to all as a matter of course. No one keeps score on who contributes what, how often, or with what significance. If credit is claimed, it is claimed for all. Certainly this is not true for all scholars, scientists, etc., but it has been more conspicuous among some of them than among other co-workers. Collaboration is also found in some families.

The essence of collaboration is "what is mine is yours when and if you need or want it" which is a far cry from the "what's yours is mine and what's mine's my own" with which all human beings begin. Collaboration is not suitable to all relationships, nor is everyone who is capable of manifesting it able to do so in all social situations. But the socially mature can and do manifest it in some particular relationships and on behalf of some collective enterprises.

The frank impulse to eliminate any others who interfere with immediate and absolute satisfactions, that characterizes the socially immature, is absent in the socially mature under ordinary circumstances. Direct attack, for example, may well revive it. Curtailment of the impulse to eliminate others, incidentally, can be a handicap for mature adults confronted by people who suffer no restraint on their impulses to destroy whatever stands in their way if they are not prevented from so doing. The disappearance of impulses to eliminate others is not only an outcome of restraint; it follows from the transformation of the experience of some particular other people as intrinsically valuable into respect for people in general. Gratification in giving satisfaction is also generalized into a predisposition to be helpful, a willingness to compromise and to cooperate.

Superordination becomes conspicuous in the associations of all adults. Parenthood places them in charge of the young. The acquisition of knowledge and skills makes them superior to those who lack them to whom they begin to transmit them, and on whose behalf they exercise them. Immature adults use their powers to dominate over others, even to eliminate them. It is the mark of the socially mature that they exercise authority with responsibility, that is, in the interests of the needs of others in their charge or the successful achievement of collective ends sought rather than for the enhancement of egocentric gratifications. This is the logical outcome of the recognition of the intrinsic significance of human beings.

The type of society and the cultural formulations widely disseminated among the population determine what forms of interaction will be most conspicuous among the adults in it. In tribal communities and what are called "authoritarian" societies, superordination and subordination characterize the relationship between men and women, parents and children, teachers and students, employers and employees, professionals and clients. Since the number of social equals in anyone's life are few in these societies, competition is rare and so is collaboration.

In highly mobile, heterogeneous societies that are culturally egalitarian, competition is very common, superordination is frequently disguised because it is often morally in disrepute; subordination, even when based on youth and ignorance, is resisted. In the United States, for example, competition is confused by cultural definition with a "law of nature" and is thought by many citizens to be a keystone for "the American way of life." The United States is quite generally referred to as a "competitive" society.

Although variations in culture determine which forms of 'interaction are likely to prevail in a society, forms of interaction are not themselves culturally determined. They are manifestations of degrees of self-regulation that result from the coercions that the necessary presence of other people exercise on individual egocentric impulses. Competition and cooperation, *et al.*, are not disembodied spirits or forces that influence mankind rather like the Furies, or the Walkyrie riding the winds. The ability to behave competitively, or cooperatively, not to mention collaboratively, with other people does not come by growth alone nor by mere verbal commands. All human beings start life so dominated by compelling somatic needs and are so lacking in the means to satisfy them, that their condition is best described as one of conflict with others. Fortunately, physical helplessness keeps the young subordinate, thereby providing their elders with the opportunity to effect the social and cultural development that enables them to live among others as adults.

There are great differences between the social resources and circumstances of adolescents and young adults. They stem primarily from the fact that young adults become responsible to and for particular other people and their maintenance, as well as their own. The experience of parenthood puts young adults at the transmitting end of social and cultural tradition. From this time on, they supply to others what up to this time they received from others. This involves a tremendous shift in the nature of their social relationships and their participation in social organizations. It reveals to them something about the complexity and significance of general social order and its connections with individual welfare. It establishes willingness to contribute to it.

Roughly, the threshold between early and middle social adulthood is marked by the end of child-bearing, where choice in this matter is possible, and the entrance of the last child into school, in complex societies, or into youth groups in tribal communities. Domestic and occupational skills are mastered. Middle age is the period in which physical powers begin to decline. They may be maintained to the end of this phase, but it is unlikely that new physical skills can be added. It is more likely that some will be lost before this phase is over.

The duration of the social phase of early adulthood is in part related to the time it takes to achieve the cultivation and knowledge required in particular social settings. It is also related to the parental history of individuals. As long as there are young children in a household it is difficult for parents greatly to expand their pursuits and relationships beyond the scope of their domestic and occupational responsibilities. But when the last child moves freely among his peers, family life changes radically. Consequently, so do relations between spouses, between parents and children, and between these and grandparents.

In societies in which kinship is not the determining factor for most relationships throughout life, middle-aged, socially mature adults tend to establish new non-family relationships in pursuit of new interests. It is the middle-aged in complex societies who initiate and maintain community projects, support artistic and intellectual activities, direct philanthropic organizations, enter into political and church administration, and so forth. Occupational achievement that assures sufficient economic resources for maintenance is another factor that frees some middle-aged individuals from the concentration of effort in this regard that was necessary in earlier years and enables them to join in other endeavors.

The life of the middle-aged is different in important respects from that of young adults. Adaptation to some losses in resources and relationships and ability to benefit from new ones requires no little effort on the part of individuals and the availability of some particular social conditions.

Middle Age

The social aspects of middle age do not involve dramatic changes. Middle age is characterized by the extension of routine associations, knowledge, and skills and the application of these personal resources to the maintenance of self, significant others, and the social order in which one lives.

The bulk of the world's work is done by the socially competent middle-aged. Although the demands upon them do not require the development of much that is conspicuously new, the maintenance of the personal integration and social competence of the middle-aged is not easy. They are called upon to cope with the young, the aged, the management of communities, the state of their societies, and whatever dislocating social and cultural changes and catastrophes that happen to occur in their time.

The middle-aged may be in the prime of their lives, but they have passed the peak of their physical prowess. By the end of this period, some physical regression is inevitable. Because this is natural and inescapable, adaptation to it often appears easy to those who view it in prospect or retrospect. Before the fact, it is not real, and after, for those who have made their peace with it, it no longer matters very much. But first encounters with the blurring of vision, the blunting of hearing, the diminution of endurance, the stiffening of muscles, and so forth, often arouse fear. These are the first intimations of mortality.

Besides, diminished physical powers have social consequences. They begin at a time when family, occupational, and social demands are heaviest. In order to meet these, many agreeable exchanges with others and many leisure activities are eliminated because there is insufficient energy for both. Only the young can habitually burn candles at both ends. This involves what Harry Stack Sullivan used to call "the grace-notes of life." Many of them disappear in middle age. Unless individuals have developed a capacity for satisfaction in giving satisfaction and satisfaction in the exercise of ability they are likely to feel hard-pressed and overworked in this phase. The socially mature find it rewarding. With maturity and competence, and some luck, middle-aged people can manage to do most of what they want to do. Few want to play basketball or climb Everest.

There is a category of people for whom the biological changes of middle life do entail strains of great personal import. These are the people whose occupations depend upon physical strength, and whose retirement, therefore, becomes mandatory for them in middle age. For professional athletes and dancers, for pilots and construction workers, etc., the disruptions that result from separation from their routine opportunities to exercise their abilities and from the interpersonal relationships associated with this can be disintegrating unless they have become mature enough to have exercised foresight and so to have provided for this change. Retirement in middle age can have the same incapacitating effects for the socially immature that it has in the next phase of human life when it is culturally as well as biologically enforced. The importance of such characteristics of mature social performance as foresight, the ability to extend skills, the capacity to apply rational processes of thought to concrete circumstances, and an end to competitiveness become clearly apparent in the last stages of human development. The body betrays everyone in time. Only domination over it by cultivated social resources make it possible to benefit from the conditions that obtain at the end of the human life-cycle.

Some of the social and cultural elaborations of sexual satisfaction and its pursuit that are found almost everywhere make middle age a source of anxiety for the immature, especially for the adolescent middle-aged. The association of physical beauty and vigor with the ideal object of sexual interest is so universal that one is almost forced to conclude that this is biologically determined, though the ideal of beauty is not. In any case, the physical inroads of middle age remove the middle-aged from the top of the list of the most sexually desirable. This is no threat to people who have moved beyond social adolescence to view members of the opposite sex as human beings, rather than as mere instruments for sexual satisfaction, and who have established stable relations with enough of them to assure their own sexual gratification. It is possible for the mature middle-aged to enjoy sex more than they did in earlier periods, but it takes social maturity for them to do so.

This possibility is not available to the socially immature individuals in the category of the middle-aged. If sexual quantity rather than quality is still an important basis for self-esteem, every new physical blemish has cultural significance that handicaps them in sexual competition and threatens their personal integration. The middle-aged Lothario and the middle-aged ingenue are figures of pity and ridicule everywhere. For the middle-aged of both sexes, sexual competition with the young is a losing game. Therefore, it is a mark of middle-aged maturity to withdraw from it.

The relationships that provide access to sexual satisfaction are not the only ones that change and require new knowledge and skill if they are to be maintained in this phase of development. Young adults are chiefly occupied with themselves and their young children and the maintenance associations that sustain them. Most young adults can still look to their parents for many kinds of assistance. The middle-aged are called upon to be responsible for the welfare of two generations, their children and their elders. Both of these have compelling needs which they cannot supply by their own efforts; the first, because they have not acquired the necessary skills and means; the second, because they have lost them.

The middle-aged are the parents of adolescents and young adults. Since adolescence is unsettling at best and the means for closing the "generation gap" are rarely easily accessible, it takes a good deal of hindsight and foresight and individual social and cultural competence for parents successfully to cope with the needs of their adolescent children. Immature parents greatly exacerbate the trials of adolescents. But success in assisting them to mature young adulthood does not release middle-aged parents from continued effort on their behalf. Weddings, financial assistance or physical maintenance until occupational stability is achieved, various kinds of support for new parents and infant grandchildren are a continuing drain on the personal, social, and material resources of the middle-aged. Satisfaction in giving satisfaction is their only major potential compensation.

At the same time, the parents of the middle-aged are aging, being forced to retire, becoming ill, and dying. Just when and how and to what extent the maintenance of elders becomes the responsibility of the middle-aged varies with the accidents of life histories, levels of personal and economic achievement, and the institutions of the societies in which people live, but few individuals escape some demands for the care of parents and none escapes the adaptations required by their death. For mature people, whatever their personal unhappiness over this event, their own lives have become sufficiently self-regulated and independent to sustain it without social disarray when their parents die. None of this is easy and all of it takes social competence.

In complex industrial societies, absorption in family and occupational relationships and activities are not permitted the mature and competent middle-aged. Their participation in organizations—community, church, political, artistic, philanthropic, educational, and so forth—is solicited by both their juniors and their elders. They constitute the keystone for social continuity. It is in this period that individuals make major direct contributions to their social orders. In a sense, and largely unwittingly for the most part, this is one of the major purposes for the elaborate cultivation that has been imposed upon them from birth. The voluntary services that make a much larger contribution to societies than is often noticed, are almost entirely manned by people in this category of population. Voluntary service that offers nothing except satisfaction in giving satisfaction depends upon the socially mature.

Although political office and the chairmanship of boards of directors, the presidency of labor unions, etc. are often well compensated and provide prestige besides, many of these activities are not part of routine maintenance occupations. The people who undertake these tasks frequently have to interrupt their occupational or professional careers and not infrequently give up material rewards and private relationships and interests to what is called community service. Furthermore, they have to be willing to extend their knowledge and augment their skills. Few young adults have the resources needed for some of the important activities required for the maintenance of societies. Few can afford the interruption of either their regular careers or family commitments. Few aging people can stand the strains that many of these activities entail. So it is the middle-aged who man policy-making and high administrative positions in all spheres of activity in societies, including those that are chiefly concerned with the maintenance of societies and their geo-political units. Not all of them are socially mature, but it often costs the population they serve a great deal, sometimes in life and limb, when they are not.

Once a full range of mental skills has been developed by an individual, the word development is not the best description of what follows. Both mental and linguistic competence for the rest of their lives depends upon the exercise of these skills and their extension to an ever-widening range of experience, communication, and intellectual analysis and creation.

This leads to a continually improved grasp of reality and more and more accurate appraisal and evaluation of people, including self. Foresight increases with hindsight and precise formulation of experience over time facilitates the relevant recall that is a large part of effective judgment. How much expansion is required for the negotiation of the demands of middle age varies with the kind of society in which people live and their places in it. But some capacity for accurate analysis of events, some knowledge of means to resolve recurring problems, and some foresight of probable consequences of what has existed and probable needs with respect to what may be is expected of the mature middle-aged anywhere.

The cultural challenge for the middle-aged is chiefly the acquisition of knowledge and skills. Arrival at maturity involves the ability to do this. Both the range and nature of the cultural requirements for this phase vary with the society and culture of individuals and their particular immediate social environment. Formal training, self-consciously applied, makes for uncertain performance. Competence involves the transformation of much early domestic and occupational learning into automatic responses: enculturation, in short. This frees individuals to seek and add knowledge as need arises. The mature middle-aged have a substantial cultural reservoir open to automatic recall.

In complex and heterogeneous societies, the expansion of relationships and activities beyond family and occupational and neighborhood associations calls for recovery from early enculturation, that is, a conscious evaluation of basic assumptions. In tribal communities or homogeneous societies what one is taught when young suffices for the rest of life. But when adults in heterogeneous societies begin to man organizations whose activities involve a wide range of their populations, tolerance for cultural difference becomes a requirement for competence.

Such tolerance begins for many in early adulthood, but it is more likely to be put to the test of practical application in the middle phase. Exchanges with people whose enculturation is significantly different demands deliberate thought about some previous assumptions. Since some anxiety is evoked by this it is a hazard for the middle-aged who are immature. For example, failure to achieve further enculturation is sometimes manifest by United States senators or representatives who have been so effective in state legislatures that they are voted into the national one. In this body, national interests frequently require the subordination of local mores, as well as interests. Some men cannot do this, not merely out of self-interest in terms of re-election, but literally because of their inability to abandon convictions that were locally engendered as part of their early enculturation. Much of the fruitless discussion in the meetings of the United Nations and of its sterility with respect to effective action stems from the same source. Many of its members cannot transcend their national enculturation in the interests of international welfare. They are still "juvenile" in their partisanship and "local" in their enculturation.

Success in overcoming individual ethnocentrism is commonly registered in what laymen call poise and sophistication. Conspicuous development of this kind is called cosmopolitanism. What is involved is transcendence over local culture. Because this achievement enhances the intrinsic value of human beings *per se*, it augments adaptation to other people. As long as only those people who are like oneself are conceived as fully human, one's range of cooperative associations is narrow. The ability to accept people who are culturally different removes arbitrary limits to the number and kind of stable and effective interpersonal relationships that a person can establish. In societies in which individual maintenance is enhanced by geographic and social mobility, this is a personal asset and a contribution to collective order and maintenance as well.

Middle age is associated with conservatism. Whether this is valued as an asset or a liability depends upon prevailing cultural formulations and existing needs for change. In any case, maturity tends to make those who achieve it conservative in some measure for several reasons. The most pervasive reason is their development of a large category of interpersonal needs, culturally defined, that regulate much of their routine behavior more automatically than not. Automatic behavior is extremely stable because it does not evoke attention. Another reason is that increased awareness of the complexity of social situations and of the limiting effects of physical, biological, and social conditions on action leads to demand for specificity in plans for change and precision in formulation of demands.

However, one mark of social maturity in middle age is sufficient freedom from anxiety in relations with others and sufficient cultural competence to enable individuals intellectually to appraise the concrete circumstances of their lives with respect to their utility for supplying satisfactions for repetitive needs, both individual and collective. Such people can recognize the need for change and use their abilities to achieve it. They are not the "old dogs" who cannot be taught "new tricks." But their stability as individuals contributes to the stability of their societies. Anarchy and perpetual revolution are the themes of abstract thought-systems dear to adolescents of any age. No society can be organized on these principles. Disorder for its own sake appeals chiefly to the childish and adolescent.

Extreme resistance to change in adults is not a sign of social maturity. On the contrary, it usually denotes juvenile dependence for personal comfort on the organization of homogeneous peers and rigid adherence to what they were taught when young. The threat of change sets off acute anxiety in them, and they mobilize their kind for defense. Anxious adult juveniles can become malevolent toward those who disturb them. Their cooperation and competitive orientation to one another depend on homogeneity and the maintenance of particular standards. When this is absent, they regress socially and the childish impulse to eliminate others who stand in their way prevails. The mature middle-aged are not made anxious by change. They have the resources to adapt to new social and cultural conditions, even to initiate them.

The competence of the socially mature middle-aged and their release from much of the competitiveness between peers that continues into young adulthood remove a great many occasions for anxiety for them. Their level of self-regulation and their pleasure in the exercise of ability detach them from direct and overt forms of external coercion. They have acquired an extensive cultural repertoire and developed the capacity for sympathy for others that transforms most of the people they encounter from mere instrumental means to ends into persons who are at least worthy of respect. These attributes are the principal coercions of mature middle-aged people. Since these are self-generated, these people have finally achieved a high degree of autonomy.

Human autonomy is always limited. Mature middle-aged adults are not independent of others for their continued well-being, and they are even more responsible for others than most people. The need to live among one's kind is a continuing and inescapable coercion. But the extension of choices that competence achieves and the substitution of self-regulation for reliance on command that are characteristic of the socially mature middle-aged provide more social latitude than was previously available to them. They do not feel pushed around by other people, nor do they experience the cultural requirements of their social milieu as intolerably arbitrary. Neither do they mistake them for laws of nature. The socially mature come to recognize at last that it is organization and culture, not people, that are instrumental.

All forms-of-interaction are available to mature young adults and so continue for middle-aged ones. But age itself shifts the pattern of their use. The mature middle-aged are more often in positions of superordination, they collaborate with more people, and they compete less than they did in earlier stages of development.

The end of the phase of social middle age brings changes that gradually move people into the next and final stage of social development, namely, old age. The loss of fertility, the physical and social maturation of children, the push of young and newly middle-aged adults in all organizations, retirement, and awareness of death are the conspicuous features that indicate that individuals have reached the threshold of old age. The comfortable negotiation of these events, and others related to them, requires the most skillful use of remaining resources by individuals. The last phase of the human life-cycle is at least as socially demanding as adolescence, and offers none of its promise.

The asset of old age is freedom, but it takes great and long effort and much good fortune to enjoy it. Except in societies such as the traditional Chinese, in which age itself was greatly honored, few people welcome old age. Some manage periodic and sometimes rueful pleasures and succeed in living through it with their dignity intact.

Old Age

In tracing stages of social development, emphasis is placed on competence for collective action and the maintenance of social institutions. Although individual well-being depends in large measure on this competence because human beings require collective order, it entails increasing interference with direct access to individual somatic satisfactions and individual impulse. In short, it involves constraint, little of which is initially accepted willingly and, therefore, which must be imposed by various means of coercion. Social maturity is achieved at the expense of somatic impulse, which is always individual and egocentric. It requires domination of the organic by conceptual interference.

In the last phase of the human life-cycle, two inescapable conditions are critically important. Organic regressions make for new efforts to transcend organic demands. These vary from individual to individual, but no one escapes some and all face the fact that the period ends with death. The second crucial factor is the gradual removal of the aging and aged from collective activities and collective settings. The rapidity and extent of this change varies for individuals, but none escapes it.

Both these conditions require extensive adaptation and management of resources by individuals, new social accomplishments. This is better described as new and careful use of previously developed resources than as development. It is doubtful that new resources are available for cultivation. This is why the felicity of individuals in old age depends so much on how successfully they have negotiated earlier stages. It takes high levels of socialization and extensive cultivation for the aged merely to maintain integration and satisfactions.

Their greatest threat is massive biological deterioration, especially regressions that involve the central nervous system, which undo them as persons. During such biological changes, the old are reduced to the kind of dependence for survival that characterizes infancy and childhood. It is a social death in advance of physical death.

But even the aged who are biologically fortunate must cope with accumulating physical limitations and incapacities. Their ability to do so depends upon how well they have succeeded in dominating organic demands in earlier stages. This manifestation of social maturity greatly augments their probable maintenance of social relationships as old people. Absorption in physical states excludes interest in other people and restricts the interest of others ·in the biologically obsessed individual as well. This augments the inescapable increase in social isolation of the old, thereby contributing to their social disintegration.

The social isolation of aging and old people is not merely an outcome of biological regression, though it is related to it. From the point of view of collective maintenance, competent socialization and enculturation of individuals are measured in terms of their ability to maintain and contribute to social organizations and cultural accumulations. By the criterion of collective utility, the inability of aging persons to keep up the quantity and pace of activity that marked the peak of their social achievement, however high its quality, is a sign of social, as well as physical, decline. In other words, from the collective point of view, old age is inevitably increasingly non-productive. In some pre-literate communities this fact was frankly revealed. The old were abandoned and left to die.

However, in complex societies, conceptual activities and their products have become increasingly important and the accumulation of knowledge and formulation of experience of the old represents an important resource for the populations in which they live. Concomitantly, expansion in the range of both socialization and enculturation in complex societies has led to widely accepted notions about treating the physically handicapped humanely, that is, as persons, whether they be infants, children, the aged, or even other animals. To this the bonds of affection must be added as an important contributing factor to collective acceptance of the right of old people to be supplied with the means and conditions required for the satisfaction of their special needs.

But the degree of this acceptance varies both among given populations and between them. No complex society includes institutional arrangements for biologically eliminating them, but few include adequate institutional arrangements for their well-being. This has been the responsibility of families for the most part until the recent past and so it has depended on individual sentiments and the resources of particular familes. The inevitable decrease in social utility that characterizes aging makes the aged prone to neglect. The neglect hastens their social decline. It even induces it in many cases in which it could have been avoided.

In societies with economies based on extensive technological development in which the majority of the population live in large cities individuals begin to age socially long before they age biologically. As participants in economic enterprises which, incidentally, are the means of maintenance for themselves and their dependents, their utility ends at an earlier and earlier age. People are literally eliminated from this sphere by enforced retirement. Autonomous nuclear families are essentially highly specialized units for child-raising. They dissolve functionally when children move out and on. This retires the majority of women in their fifties and in societies in which these families prevail few of them will be compensated by grandparental relationships and functions. This relationship is highly problematic in modern industrial societies. Geographic and social mobility keep many grandparents strangers to their grandchildren. Furthermore, autonomous nuclear families do not have sufficient resources to provide for aging elders. More and more of them are exiled from family settings and there are few appropriate other arrangements in these societies to compensate them.

Yet, to quote from Enid Bagnold's play *The Chalk Garden*, people "who are alive have to be somewhere." While alive there are resources at the command of individuals some of which are uniquely available to the old who are not biologically undone. Of these, wisdom is, perhaps, the most collectively valuable.

It should be clear that the social phase of old age is at least as demanding and can be as disruptive to individual well-being as adolescence. Like adolescence, the fate of individuals in old age depends greatly on biological factors. The healthy functioning of the body is a great advantage for the maintenance of personal integration and interpersonal relationships. Severe physical handicaps often interfere with the integrative faculties (whatever these are) and, further, by making individuals dependent on others for physical care, may seriously limit the exercise of their social abilities. Most important of all, clear awareness and increasing probability of death is at least as difficult to integrate into the social life and personal organization of aging individuals as lust and the capacity for reproduction are for adolescents. It is probably much more difficult; since death is the end of person as well as organism, the approach to it involves progressive loss of organic powers, social relationships, and personal satisfactions. The recognition of these inescapable changes is scarcely a source of personal security. The strains of adolescents are associated with great potential expansion of personal resources, social relationships, and achievements and the creation of life. Surely these are easier prospects to integrate than a series of inescapable losses and death. Personal breakdown in old age is at least as common as in adolescence and by no means all of it is due to organic disintegration.

Like all stages of development, comfortable adaptation by individuals to the physical and social conditions of aging depends upon previous development, access to personal relationships, and prevailing cultural formulations. Age differs sharply from other stages in that it is not a preparation for ensuing phases. The old have no future to provide for. Therefore, the conspicuous advantage for the mature and fortunate among the old is freedom, but, for everyone, it requires expert use of their remaining resources and adaptation to drastic physical and interpersonal changes to benefit from the assets of age.

Biologically, age begins with the loss of fertility. In this respect there are conspicuous differences between men and women. Typically, loss of fertility occurs much earlier in the life-cycle of women than of men. This does not mean that at fifty women become crones with no pleasurable options between that time and the grave. But their mates, unless these are twenty or so years older, are still fertile and this gives them choices that women do not have. They cannot, like their fifty-year-old counterparts, have a second chance to apply the knowledge and skills and material resources that they have accumulated to a second family cycle, for example. At fifty, a man is still biologically middle-aged; a woman is moved into the category of the old by inescapable biological conditions.

This biological difference between males and females has important social consequences. Sexually, women are apt to lose access to satisfactions long before they lose the impulse for them. Almost everywhere, the pursuit of twenty-year-old males by women in their forties and fifties is considered ridiculous, the reverse is not. It is exceptional for twenty-year-old males to court fifty-year-old women, but twenty-year-old females are often attracted by fifty-year-old males. Biologically, this makes sense. The social response reflects the fact that at fifty men can mate and beget and women cannot.

The fact that women age earlier than men accounts for some of the greatest strains of the initial phase of aging for both. Unless husbands and wives have achieved the maturity that involves the domination of biological impulses by those that are the result of their social development, in societies in which custom and law make it possible, this is the period in which immature husbands are prone to break up marriages of long standing and to pursue their adolescent romantic ideals in a new marriage. The women they marry are often no older than their daughters and the children of these marriages are often younger than some of their grandchildren.

Socially, this is obviously unfair. Not only have fifty-year-old wives a long record of services rendered, they have no prospect of appropriate compensation or substitution. Whatever material compensation they get is less than a new wife will have access to, and their chances of acquiring new husbands or even sexual partners are slim.

Because the personal and private lives of adults are overwhelmingly organized around couples, the loss of male partners at the beginning of old age is devastating for women in other ways. It breaks up family circles in which many have lived all their lives. At best, then, children have two centers that demand attention, which disperses it. At worst, they take sides and not all favor their mothers. It also breaks up circles of friends and acquaintances that have been the second line of interpersonal support for these women. Single women, especially aging and abandoned ones, are a social liability in most societies. A newly married couple is not. Gradually these women are often condemned to an unavoidable kind of social isolation at precisely the time when they are least able to cope with it. Not a few disintegrate. It is true that the functional disintegration of family and social circles is inescapable by the end of this phase in all societies that are not dominated by very large extended families. But there is all the difference in the world between facing something that is shared by everyone, and coping with a situation that is not, even though it may not be uncommon.

The loss of fertility may have other consequences in societies in which child-bearing is highly valued and associated with high social prestige, because family continuity is important. In societies in which this is the case—traditional Chinese, for example—infertile women can be abandoned to what amounts to social non-existence, unless protected by bonds of affection and cultural bonds of obligation from the young to the old.

Other conspicuous physiological regressions are inescapable in old age. It is in this regard that one can properly speak of "luck." How much regression, what kind, how incapacitating, depend upon biology alone. Severe biological invasions can lead to a resurgence of the domination of an individual by his somatic needs and a return to great social dependency. In such cases, physical regression is accompanied by social regression.

Finally, the aging are confronted with death, not only their own, but that of their contemporaries. Up to middle age, most people consider the possibility of their own death unreal. Young people usually consider death for their grandparent's generation natural, and they respond to the death of their peers, and even that of young parents, as an exceptional occurrence. But there comes a moment when awareness that each individual life-course has an end becomes vivid. It may be that this begins with the death of parents. Certainly, by the time people move into the category of the aged, the probabilities with respect to death cannot be ignored.

The death of peers results in increasing social isolation with all its results. Foreseeable limitation to the number of years of an individual's life expectancy alters many of his activities. Long-term ventures cannot reasonably be undertaken. As age increases, life begins to be lived within a framework of immediate circumstances. In this respect, the aged and children have much in common, though for very different reasons. Children have no foresight and are not aware of their probable future. The foresight of the aged reveals that their future is limited and uncertain. Whatever long-term planning they may do can only be realistically oriented to their descendants.

Acceptance of and adaptation to these biologically induced circumstances require either a high level of social and cultural cultivation, with its concomitant reservoir of individual resources, or extremely fortunate social and cultural insulation. In some tribal communities and in societies dominated by Confucian culture, for example, age itself has been so greatly honored that even incompetent individuals could be sustained at whatever levels of social development they had achieved. But in societies in which independent self-regulation is the prerequisite for benefits from the social order, both materially and personally, only the aging who can transcend their increasing physical disabilities and maintain their personal integration and interpersonal skills can hope to avoid devastating social isolation.

Effective adaptation to age in most modern societies can be achieved only by the extensive development of mental and linguistic resources, including literacy. It is at the end of life that the very great importance of mental development and extensive enculturation to individual social competence is clearly apparent. These are the only means the aging have available to compensate for their loss of physical prowess and mobility.

Again, how well each individual does, depends on an element of "luck." Even the highly cultivated can be brought down by physical ailments that attack their central nervous systems. But if this does not happen, age can actually augment the mental and linguistic resources of people. A long memory based on wide experience and freedom from the necessity to hedge for a long future can improve judgment. Independence from the approvals and disapprovals of others removes sources of anxiety for the aged and, hence, of interference with higher mental functions.

It is the aged who *can* attain wisdom. Age does not guarantee it, but it is a condition for it. Wisdom is distinguished from expert knowledge, which even the relatively young and immature may have, by a factor of judgment; and good judgment depends upon some measure of detachment and a sense of proportion. The appearance of these traits depends not only on long experience, which in itself does not produce them, but upon a degree of actual social withdrawal from associations that are linked to individual maintenance and that of dependents, or to the fulfillment of long-term projects. Only the aging are likely to be in this social position. It requires precise formulation of experience as well, not mere endurance.

The inescapable loss of interpersonal relationships and active membership in many organizations that goes with old-age is most readily compensated for by access to mediated sources of interpersonal enrichment. This is the reason for the great importance of literacy for old people in complex industrial societies. Radio and television can also be of use in this respect, though neither have approached the range and depth of resources available to the literate. Ability to communicate to others freely and precisely in writing is another important means available to the cultivated elderly for maintaining relationships with surviving peers and family members. The telephone is an additional aid in technologically developed societies. Finally, old people who speak and write well or who manifest skills that depend on literacy often attract young people to them and succeed in adding some new relationships to their diminishing associations. People who have cultivated skills in intellectual and linguistic activities have the advantage over those who have not when they are aging and old. Physical decline forces them to give up activities that depend upon physical stamina. The withdrawal from such activities can actually augment the opportunities for the elderly to exercise abilities in intellectual and linguistic fields.

Increase in social isolation is inevitable for the aged. The social distance between the young and the old is very great. In this respect, the old are also not unlike adolescents. They too are aware of a "generation gap" and in their case it will never be bridged. Few, if any, young people can believe in the one-time vigor of the elderly. They cannot imagine their arthritic grandfathers on the football field or their grandmothers leading a college prom in the equivalent of the latest dance craze. That either ever had anything to do with the sexual urges and excitements and gratifications being newly experienced by adolescents is unthinkable for them. And so, the immediate active preoccupations of the young and the old do not meet. Even the exploits of a Napoleon, or a Nelson, or a Lenin, or a Columbus, or a "Moon" man are more apt to be a bore to their grandchildren than not. At the same time, the "growing pains" of the young generations become remote to the old. They have experienced the cycle and shared it with others too many times. Most of all, important new cultural innovations that will determine much in the lives of the young, but will not affect those of the old, are not very interesting to the latter. These factors separate the old from most of the youngest generation that has grown beyond infancy and childhood.

Retirement separates the old from their peers and from the opportunity to exercise their most extensively cultivated skills. Because the better part of the lives of most people is organized around their occupations, domestic for the majority of women, the disintegration of the arrangements, schedules, and associations in this sphere is a severe threat to the personal integration of all but the highly cultivated.

This is especially true when it is involuntary. In modern industrial societies, enforced retirement at increasingly lower ages is becoming more and more widespread. Although increases in "fringe benefits" and pensions are designed to protect the old from physical hardship, no financial assistance can solve the problem of social isolation.

Somatic handicaps begin to remove the elderly from physical mobility. When it becomes difficult to walk or to care for physical needs away from home, people are literally out of circulation. In the large cities of industrial societies this easily leads to a condition resembling solitary confinement. Small towns still provide a certain amount of informal "dropping in" as people "go by." At least people do not drop out of sight in small communities as they do in cities. But a move to small towns is not a solution for many urban aged because it cuts them off from the family and familiar relationships that are their principal source of interpersonal support.

Finally, the death of peers continuously diminishes the social circle of the aged. It is not only the death of the people they have known personally that is involved. The aging and the aged read the obituary columns with a kind of masochistic, but intense, interest. Beside the "there but for the grace of God go I" reaction, the old keep score of the surviving public figures of their time. The names and faces of the political, religious, scientific, artistic, literary, theatrical, and athletic scenes of their prime years begin to disappear. The wider social realm in which the old have lived by conceptual means becomes depopulated and as this happens it ceases to have any significant reality for many of them.

These factors are a serious threat to the well-being of the old. Only the socially mature and physically lucky can overcome them. These relatively few in any population use detachment from routine as an opportunity to do many things for which they had little time in their middle years. They cannot replace their contemporaries, but they are able to establish some friendly relationships with people younger than themselves. Such elderly people reap some rewards from past efforts to cultivate their personal resources.

The cultural formulations that particularly affect the old

are those that determine general attitudes toward them in the people among whom they live. If age is honored, the old will be.

For socially mature old persons, biology is the chief coercion. Physical regression and particular physical handicaps can force dependency upon them and begin to rule their lives. Foresight of death compels preparations for it. Otherwise, there is little that can coerce the old. They cease to be subject to the approvals and disapprovals of others for what they need and ostracism can hardly be used as a threat to people whose peers are few and whose active participation in collective enterprises has already ended. Responsibility has usually been passed on to the next generation. What is left is freedom. In short, the old who are not seriously handicapped physically and who have adequate personal resources are socially less constrained than other people.

Physical disabilities may reduce the old to relationships that are predominantly ones of superordination and subordination. This is one of the conditions that evokes analogies between old age and childhood. The quality of these exchanges is utterly different for the very young and the old, but the helplessness of the latter may make them as dependent as the young and can be as dominating an influence on those who care for them.

Subordination is not common for the vigorous and mature elderly. Most exchanges between adults are in the mode of voluntary cooperation and this is true for the old, but the really competent among them are increasingly the superiors in superordinate-subordinate relationships. The absence of peers eliminates competition for them, except in games, perhaps. The ideal-typical elder who is socially mature and extensively enculturated is the *éminence grise*, a peerless member of a population, not merely first among equals.

The welfare of the aged, like that of social adolescents, depends very greatly on the cultural conditions in which it is lived. In populations in which age is associated with wisdom and the relations between the old and the young are characterized by respect and gratitude, the old are routinely provided with what they need with no damage to their self-esteem. Under these circumstances, their personal integration often survives even physical disabilities; and a viable set of relationships that make those between grandparents and grandchildren of great affective value often provides the old with opportunities to exercise their abilities and even to expand them. In societies in which age not only is not worthy of respect, but viewed as a sign of inferiority, neither proper physical care nor sustaining personal relationships are provided many old people. Early retirement is enforced and deprives many able-bodied and extremely competent people of the opportunity to exercise their abilities. Children all but abandon parents, once they reach early adulthood. Grandparents are often strangers to their grandchildren. These cultural and interpersonal conditions offer no support for the personal maintenance of the old and the rates of disintegration among them under these conditions are high.

It is obvious that the general consequences of aging for populations will vary with the cultural and social circumstances that are readily available to the old among them. If they prosper, the old are a rich source of knowledge, even of wisdom. If they are inadequately provided for, they become a burden on particular individuals and on collective resources. The cost is not merely material.

Conclusion

The fact that the achievement of social maturity by every individual is a long and complicated development and that human mortality makes it a transitory collective commodity has important social implications. The products of human collective life that are subsumed under the word *culture* can be preserved and, hence, accumulate. The abilities that individual human beings develop that enable some of them to maintain the collective order on which human life and the fulfillment of human potentialities depend vanish with them.

Every infant is destined to repeat this long cycle if he is to achieve social as well as physical maturity. A large proportion of the resources of every population must be devoted to providing the conditions for this development. The discrepancy between the record of cultural advances in human history and the repetition of social incompetence for relationships between people that promote individual and general welfare is conspicuous. Cultural sophistication does not guarantee sustaining interpersonal relationships or civility for populations. Only the extensive social development of a large proportion of each generation does that.

Since social development is never in the category of "finished business" for individuals or populations, advance in this respect can stem only from improvement in the understanding of what it entails and collective effort to provide the conditions that are essential to it.

Chapter Eight

Some General Connections between Individual Social Development and Social Organizations: Socialization

IT SHOULD BE APPARENT that the social and cultural competence of adults is not achieved simply by the imposition of factors that are alien to human life upon recalcitrant and resistant human organisms, nor are social attributes superficial traits. Social maturity is attained by the cultivation of resources that are potentially available through growth to all but the defective by people in whom these have already been cultivated. Particular kinds of relationships and organizations and a supply of cultural items are essential to this development, which is not in any sense an outcome of psychobiological potential and growth alone, but which is not independent of it. Not only is somatic development no guarantee for the development of social and cultural attributes in human beings, even though it requires them, but somatic impulses resist the complications induced by cultural modification, thereby making the social and cultural development of human beings dependent upon coercions by other people for many years of life.

Human beings are inescapably interdependent. They do not live together by choice alone. Individual satisfactions and security depend upon regular access to others. Yet, individual ability to establish and maintain stable relationships with others depends upon the maturation and cultivation of abilities that are complex, require long periods of time for development, are not guaranteed by somatic

164

growth, and are often not developed in some adult individuals at all.

Social development occurs in a series of stages, not sharply divided from one another, but discernible nonetheless. Infants cannot be cultivated to do socially and culturally what children do, or children what juveniles can do, or all three what young adults can do, any more than they can achieve physical skills prematurely. This serial aspect of social development results from its dependence upon psychobiological development. If the acquisition of cultural additions to psychobiological structure and functions and the social skills that result from adaptation to the presence of other people were not so dependent, there is no apparent reason why most of this should appear in stages at all. If these were merely a part of psychobiological growth, the two series would be one and there would be no discrepancy between the somatic and social maturation of human beings. In fact, they are interdependent and mutually influencing though neither one guarantees the other.

The processes involved in social development are complex and the conditions necessary for its achievement both numerous and beyond the control of individuals themselves. Therefore, a great many adults reach physical maturity without reaching social maturity, however this may be defined. Variation in the social skills of adults in a population is great and this fact has collective significance. The stability of organizations and their efficiency depend in large part upon how capable their members are of maintaining stable relationships and what kind of relationships. The amount of supervision and the extent of need for agents to enforce the rules on which an organization is based depend upon the levels of self-regulation of the people who man them. Whatever the occupational skills that are used in a society for the maintenance of its citizens, and of the society itself, their supply depends upon the cultivation of the conceptual potential of its members in particular ways and their enculturation of a particular kind. In a substantial percentage of the populations of what are called "underdeveloped" countries, it is the absence of a special kind of cultivation common in industrial societies that is, perhaps, the greatest impediment to their rapid technical rehabilitation.

I have presented the stages of social development of individuals as they can occur alongside stages of psychobiological growth, because it seems to me this is the best way to reveal some of the essential characteristics of the stages themselves. If one knows what abilities tend to go with what stages, it is possible to identify the different levels of social competence that characterize particular adult individuals. If one can do this, one is able to evaluate and predict what they are able to do in collective situations. Finally, if one can identify the social skills of adult individuals one can foresee that some collective results from their associations are more probable than others. The collapse of governments set up by colonial powers in the image of their own parliamentary and representational political arrangements in the "new societies" whose populations were still predominantly organized in tribes need not have been as surprising and disappointing as it has been.

The rough, ideal-typical series of stages presented here includes a few of what I consider to be basic ingredients in the social development of everyone and some of the essential social characteristics of individuals that follow from their combinations. The essential ingredients fall into the major categories I have indicated: psychobiological resources, conceptual and linguistic resources, particular interpersonal relationships and organizations, and cultural resources. This scheme is designed to cover developments that are required for life in very large and complex societies and so it includes some factors that can be eliminated, or that would at least take different forms and significance, for people who live in less complex societies.

After the early years of life, the patterns of social development necessary to attain social competence for particular individuals depend upon the kind of society in which they will be expected to live. We do not know the upper limits of what human beings might achieve. At any given time we use the most complexly developed people known to us as a standard for what is possible. It is, perhaps, justifiable to conclude that people who have not evolved to these upper limits are less socially mature in relation to species possibilities even though they are socially competent as adults in their own societies. One knows that they would not be if they moved into a more complex one and one knows that human beings are capable of more complex development.

In any case, it is clear that there are inevitable and reciprocal connections between individual social maturity and the social and cultural matrix in which it evolves. There are some developments that are universally required for adult competence, others may not be. With respect to these, one can say that if the social situations in which individuals will live as adults are of such and such a level of complexity, these additional factors will then have to characterize their later stages of development to ensure their competence.

The major social characteristics that result from combinations of these ingredients fall into two major categories which have long been recognized among social scientists and are reflected in their use of the terms *socialization*[1] and *enculturation*. The first is the word that is usually employed by sociologists, the second by anthropologists. Usage has been confusing principally because both sociologists and anthropologists have used one word to cover two major sets of processes, conditions, and the social traits they induce. In my opinion, understanding of the social development of human beings can be greatly facilitated by clearly differentiating between the referents to these terms. In life, they are concomitant and intertwined. They continually influence each other. However, they are not identical. The ingredients and conditions for social development and the evolution of social traits as a result of their mutual effects that have been traced here for the entire human life-cycle are essential referents of both these terms. Differentiating between them is one way of summarizing the two major aspects of the social development of human beings in general that result from the particular experience of each of them with other people and culture. Neither socialization nor enculturation alone constitutes the social development of human beings. In combination, they account for most of it.

[1] John A. Clausen, (ed.), *Socialization and Society* (Boston: Little, Brown & Co., 1968), is a good review of current meaning of socialization.

Socialization

All the factors that go into the transformations that enable each person who reaches adult competence to live in stable associations with people in pairs, groups, and large and complex organizations I call socialization. This especially involves the dependence of individuals on other people in a series of particular relationships which are themselves largely determined by the degrees of the helplessness of individuals to attain satisfactions for the needs associated with particular stages of growth. The interpersonal associations that appear to be essential for the socialization of everyone are mothering ones, family groups, juvenile peergroups, matings with the opposite sex, friendship pairs and intrinsic peer-groups.

These associations can only be maintained in a matrix of more organizational complexity, a tribal community or a society, and a fair proportion of the populations of communities or societies must be cultivated to a level at which they grasp their significance for individual welfare and the requirements for their maintenance. People must be capable of curtailing their individual impulses in the interest of their communities or societies.

The nature of a society is not easy to grasp. Despite much that has been written about individuals "confronting" their societies or "dropping out" of them, the fact is that no one encounters his society as a whole and no one drops out of it unless he emigrates. Unlike communities that are based on kinship and locality, societies are too large, heterogeneous, and complexly organized for an individual to experience their totality directly. The nature of a society has to be grasped conceptually on the basis of inferences from limited experience at best. Thus, children cannot understand what a society is because their conceptual abilities are not sufficiently developed to deal with such abstract synthesis and many adults do not understand the nature of their societies because their conceptual abilities have not been sufficiently cultivated, or their relevant experience is too meager, or both. It is the need for extensive ability to grasp the nature of realities that can be known only in the abstract that makes the attainment of social maturity more difficult for people who live in complex societies than for those who live in communities. More of their potential must be transformed into manifest ability for competent life in them.

For all people, the nature of the largest organization of which they are a part is gradually brought to their attention by the series of intermediate associations that have been indicated. People who live in communities can experience them directly, once their conceptual abilities have matured. But people in complex societies cannot. However, in both instances, it is the intermediate associations that cultivate abilities for the various forms of interaction with others, not membership in community or society *per se*.

These abilities appear in serial order and depend upon the powers of others to control the efforts of growing individuals to eliminate anyone who stands in the way of their absolute satisfactions and to grab all of whatever they can attain without regard for the needs of others. Everyone begins life so dominated by biological needs that he is inevitably in what amounts to a state of conflict with others because somatic impulses themselves are always egocentric. At the same time, the complete inability of everyone in the early years of life to satisfy his own needs enables the people around him to limit his conflict, indeed, to force him to compromise, thus terminating conflict and leading to some stable form of interaction. This sequence is true for people of all ages and stages of development. When conflict intervenes and interrupts relations between people its resolution always involves compromise by all participants. Unless they can withdraw from one another, this must lead to stabilization of their associations in some patterned form, or forms, of interaction. Each form of interaction in the series represents a greater degree of limitation on impulse for absolute satisfaction, limitation that depends upon direct coercion by others, or clear indication that they can be applied, up to the level of pre-adolescent social development, and upon self-regulation which is thereafter achieved by the conceptual interference of individuals themselves with their somatic impulses.

As regulation of impulse that is the result of the particular coercions of others in specified relationships increases—

control of access to satisfactions, increase and decrease in tenderness, systematic approvals and disapprovals associated with rewards and punishments, and ostracism—self-regulation evolves in response to progressive changes in the significance of other people to each maturing individual. In the beginning, mothering ones are experienced as vague presences that facilitate or impede satisfactions. These are gradually differentiated and recognized as individuals who are sources of particular satisfactions and dissatisfactions. In time, the presence of numerous others is identified as a necessary source of satisfactions, not merely as an arbitrary interference. Then, some people come to have intrinsic value, a source of satisfaction in themselves, not merely for what they can provide. Finally, the intrinsic value of some people is generalized into a recognition of the fact that all human beings are more alike than different, and that all have similar essential needs. This is what is meant by a sense of humanity. When this happens to individuals they have covered the full range of socialization. Sympathy and satisfaction in giving satisfaction to others become the principal coercions on impulses for egocentric and exclusive satisfactions. Self-regulation has become largely automatic and, therefore, dependable.

In tribal communities, or for people who live in relatively isolated and usually agrarian settlements in large, but traditional, non-industrial societies, this sequence is sufficient for adult competence to operate in and maintain collective order. These communities and societies are conceived as extensions of families. Relationships are determined by kinship and locality, for the most part. This is what is behind such terms as *motherland, fatherland, homeland*, behind the conception of fellow-citizens as *brothers* and of the authorities in the societies as *fathers*. But this relatively simple extension of the experience from birth to physical maturity dominated by family circles to the society as a whole is both false and inadequate for people who live in complex, highly technological, heterogeneous societies. Citizens of the United States, for example, do not think of their "country" as a "Motherland" or "Fatherland." The attachment of Americans to their society is too complex for such terms to be applicable. The socialization of people in complex industrial societies requires something more than adaptation to living in direct reciprocities with others.

Sociologists have long noted that modern industrial societies depend upon contractual, impersonal relationships as well as on personal ones. The larger and more technically developed the society is, the greater the number of contractual relationships between its adult citizens. For these relationships to be stable and productive, the individuals who participate in them must be capable of high levels of self-regulation and of dealing civilly with strangers. A contract cannot be enforced by external coercion. Its fulfillment depends upon the voluntary compliance of those who contract it. They may be "persuaded" by coercion, or threat of it, to comply, though reluctantly, but any time a party to a contract simply says "no," the activities prescribed by the contract will cease, even though the individuals suffer punishment thereby. This fact has been generously illustrated by illegal strikes in recent years. Essentially, contractual relationships and activities must be voluntary.

The voluntary cooperation called for, that does not need sporadic reinforcement by threats of coercion, can be acquired in juvenile peer-groups and a great many people everywhere are capable of it. Childish people are not socially capable of maintaining contractual relationships without routine supervision with its potential use of coercions. The problem that arises when socially juvenile adults enter into contractual arrangements is a result of their incapacity to extend their self-regulation to people who differ from them in any conspicuous way. So long as their contracts are with their own kind of people, or so long as they continue to see immediate advantages to themselves in the arrangement, juvenile types are dependable.

But in large and heterogeneous populations in modern industrial societies, the contractual associations between citizens are numerous. More and more of them earn their livings, are educated, and seek their diversions in corporate organizations in which membership is always contractual. The citizens of these societies are increasingly involved in encounters with representatives of governments as these become welfare states and planning organizations for their populations. Citizenship is becoming a series of contracts with governments: for military service, for taxes, for driving cars, and building buildings, for importing and exporting goods, for hunting and fishing, for medical care, for pensions, and so on and on. These are no longer services to a personal political leader or agreements between private persons who select one another for social as well as service reasons.

People in stable and particular associations are always an important part of the means to individual satisfactions and security. In modern industrial societies, the number needed by each individual has increased. Citizens in these societies depend on many people for limited services and goods, in contrast to people in tribal communities or traditional societies who depend on few people for a great deal. People in complex societies have access to a much wider range of goods and services, and the limited and specialized nature of their contracts with one another increase their social freedom and, in a measure, their social security. Dependence on a few for much is risky and limiting. But the social price required of individuals for this collective improvement is the need to reach higher levels of social development to sustain it. It requires both more deliberate thought and more self-regulation. It also requires the development of a sense of humanity that curbs partisanship. The majority of people that citizens of large, industrial societies deal with daily are strangers, though some are familiar, and they manifest a great variety of social characteristics.

The ability to tolerate strangers requires socialization that family-oriented upbringing cannot provide. So long as human beings are young and immature, they are protected from strangers. In many places they are trained to shun them, threatened with dire consequences if they have anything to do with them when they encounter them. In tribal communities and traditional societies, hostility toward strangers is more often customary than not for everyone. The adaptation of individuals to the people among whom they live in these social situations, their socialization, not only fails to develop techniques for dealing with strangers, but explicitly cultivates impulses to eliminate them, and includes instructions for so doing and enforces them by threats that ensure that the appearance of a stranger will trigger great anxiety. In these social circumstances, even the most highly socialized and self-regulating and humane individuals in a population are not only free to treat strangers in much the same way that infants and children would treat all others if they could, but are trained to do so.

Everywhere, in fact, there are determinable social boundaries that separate the people who are recognized as fellow human beings, not necessarily equal, but at least human, from people who are inferior, not quite human, or not human at all. The socialization of the young aimed at the cultivation in them of respect for some people and love for others has not been focused on all mankind, despite a good many claims that "all men are brothers." Humanity, let alone brotherhood, is ascribed only to some categories of mankind by all peoples. At best, perhaps one can say that for a few people more of mankind is considered human than not. However, saints have been notorious for exterminating heretics, church fathers for exterminating nonbelievers, and political leaders for exterminating those of their fellow citizens who did not espouse their version of truth and social justice for all mankind.

The social adaptations that constitute socialization have always been applied to people of particular social designations only. The ability that some human beings have for torturing others must stem either from lack of socialization (infants and children would be able if they physically could) or from the fact that their victims belong to a social category that is not included within the boundaries of their social restraint, or both. Even legal killing in war has to be justified by defining the enemy as wicked and socially inferior. Contests with equals are competitions, not conflict. They operate according to rules voluntarily honored, and they are not organized for the elimination of the participants.

The social conditions that modern technology has created make the practice of directing the socialization of the young to be applied only to particular kinds of people inadequate for individuals and dangerous to mankind. In large heterogeneous societies and in a social world which for the first time in history is coterminous with the globe, the social restraints exercised on behalf of others that are the manifestations of socialization must apply to all human beings despite their social variations in the interest of human survival. In the modern world, kinship and locality encompass the social relationships of fewer and fewer people. The security of the majority is dependent upon associations with strangers. Peaceful and productive relations between them demand what Cooley called "cooperation without friendship,"[2] to which one must add, without kinship.

For this, the young, who grow up best in personal associations, whether in families or in schools, churches, play groups, and so forth, need to be further cultivated to include strangers in their social range of self-regulation and to adapt to the social relationships that characterize large and complex organizations, such as corporations, large administrative organizations and the large, heterogeneous, industrialized societies in which these proliferate. The social skills needed cannot be acquired in families or other groups alone. It is both fraudulent and ineffective to try to persuade or coerce individuals to conceive of themselves as part of a "family of General Motors" or as having "a friend at Chase Manhattan." Neither these corporations nor any other are designed to perform the functions or provide the satisfactions made available in families and friendships. They provide other things that families and friends cannot provide, and they require very different social skills from their members and clients in order to do so.

People in corporate or any other large organizations must be strangers to one another if large organizations are to survive and to produce what they were organized to do. As more and more of the productive activity of people in modern industrial societies takes place in corporate and large administrative organizations, complaints about their impersonality and the instrumental nature of the associations that characterize them abound. In my opinion this results from a misreading of the nature of these organizations and what social skills they require of the people who

[2] Charles H. Cooley, *Social Organization* (New York: Schocken, 1962).

participate in them. Whether or not people can be comfortable in large organizations, or use or man them efficiently, depends upon their level of socialization. Experience in pairs and groups is insufficient training for participation in them. Large organizations such as corporations and large administrative organizations are not simply groups grown large. They are something else and these organizational techniques must be mastered just as the techniques for effective participation in groups or skill for intimacy in pairs must be cultivated.

Increase in the number of people who require goods or services, or who are needed to produce and distribute particular goods or services, which makes it impossible for all of them to meet in direct reciprocities to achieve their ends, makes group organization inadequate to achieve the ends envisaged and requires new organizational techniques.

These fall into the category usually labeled "large organizations." There is a tendency to discuss large organizations as though they are all alike. They have some features in common that distinguish them from groups, in which all members can meet to carry on their business, which are usually imprecisely called "small organizations." The large/small division is too crude to be of much use for understanding a good many important sociological conditions and events. There are categories of large organizations that differ significantly from one another, as well as from other forms of organization. Corporations are not the same as large administrative organizations, or guilds, for example. None of these organizations is the same as societies, which are the most complex social organizations so far evolved. But the socialization that enables individuals to operate effectively in corporations is a step toward competent ability to participate effectively in other large organizations. Since these are becoming the most numerous large organizations in modern societies, the social skills necessary for participation in them are an important prerequisite for the kind of socialization required for comfortable and competent membership in other large organizations.[3]

---

[3] Peter M. Blau, *Bureaucracy in Modern Society* (New York: Random House, 1956); Wilbert E. Moore, *The Conduct of the Corporation* (New York: Random House, 1962).

The most conspicuous organizational features of corporations, and all large organizations, follow from the impossibility in such organizations for all members to meet in effective direct reciprocities to achieve the ends for which they are organized. This condition requires the introduction of specific organizational techniques.

First, there are specialized executives and administrators who, in combination, determine and preside over divisions of labor and authority among members of corporations. They also serve as a kind of "switchboard" for the membership. By transmitting and receiving information and messages, they coordinate the multiple activities of many people, most of whom never see or speak to one another. Secondly, the number of operations necessary to produce the kinds of goods and services that corporations deal with, and to distribute them, makes a prescribed and elaborate division of labor among members essential. A high degree of specialization characterizes corporations. Thirdly, both large numbers of people and the large number and variety of activities involved in corporations require clearly defined divisions of authority, not only between executives and administrators and all others, but among the people who perform the activities necessary to achieve the prescribed ends. Corporations require a detailed ranking order, a hierarchy. Fourthly, the same conditions make it imperative in corporations to define clearly the purposes of the organization, the means to be used to achieve them, and the conditions for membership including requirements for positions, distribution of benefits and obligations, and sanctions for failure to keep contracts. These must be formulated and made known to corporation members and clients before the corporation begins to operate, and changes and innovations must be announced previous to their introductions.

These techniques of organization result in particular characteristics for membership in them. The smallest operational unit of large organizations is a group, limited in its potential manifestations as a group by inclusion in the larger organization. Individual people, as such, are merely sources of energy, skills, or knowledge needed to fill prescribed "positions," that is, to perform particular acts that are small links in a large chain made up of a number of acts. Nothing else about the members is organizationally relevant to this kind of organization. This, plus the anonymity that is characteristic of participation in large gatherings of people, results in the impersonality that is so conspicuously associated with membership in large organizations. Persons become personnel.

It should be clear that corporate organizations are vastly different from groups and that the social ability to operate effectively in the one does not insure ability to participate effectively in the other. The very partial involvement of each in a large organization in its total enterprise, the prescribed assignment of tasks to positions, the prescribed hierarchical arrangement of positions, and the emphasis on impersonal determination of relationships and interactions make participation in them the nearest to the role-playing of actors.

But role-playing does not involve what we have described as relationship. A role is essentially a unit of organization, a division of labor and authority with its cultural elaborations. For an actor in the theater, a role is the work he contributes to the enactment of a play by a cast—a group. It is not an autonomous group. It is part of a larger organization which, in the case of motion picture or television actors, may be a group unit of a corporation. The enactment of a play is the purpose for which the cast is assembled. The play and its requirements are known. Membership in the cast is determined by the professional skills of each actor for meeting the demands of the script. Whether or not an individual can enact the role depends upon his or her previous cultivation as an actor. Whether or not he or she will be retained in the cast also depends upon ability to cooperate with directors and fellow actors, most of whom are strangers, and most of whom remain strangers, though familiar ones, even after a two-year run of the play. The satisfactions provided by membership in the cast are various. For most actors, acquisition of means for maintenance and the satisfaction in the exercise of ability are conspicuous.

Participation in the group units of corporations is very similar. Each person is selected because he has previously acquired certain particular skills and is capable of cooperation with strangers. His returns are chiefly means for maintenance and the exercise of abilities. Like actors in a cast, the members of corporations learn some new things on their jobs that may, in time, enable them to enact other roles. But none of this inherently entails personal relationships with the people they cooperated with while filling their roles. All that this requires is sufficient cultural skill to master some particular techniques and social skill to cooperate willingly with strangers.

In fact, personal relationships do arise in large organizations, but they are discouraged. Conspicuous turnover of members, transfers, and the actual limitations on personal exchanges that participation in large organizations impose, result in a high degree of the impersonality that executives, whether of economic or religious or political organizations, desire in the interest of organizational efficiency. It is also true that some aspects of the roles or job patterns people enact, especially if they are enacted over long periods of time, become part of the repertoire of culture and skills that regulate the automatic responses of the people who enact them. Some roles and some jobs become part of their socialization and enculturation, in short. This is less true of professional actors than of members of corporations; few become Hamlets or Ophelias, whereas the occupational skills and knowledge and values, *et al.*, associated with jobs, sometimes do become part of the personal repertoire of the people who fill them. But even this does not necessarily involve personal relationships with fellow workers, and usually does not. The satisfactions derived from direct personal relationships in which each participant has important instrumental significance, if not intrinsic value, and for which role aspects are far less important than personal ones, are not to be expected from corporate social settings.

However, corporate and other large organizations can provide a large number of goods and services for a great many people, which is something no pair or group can do. Because of their high degree of division of labor and authority, which makes replacements of personnel relatively easy, these organizations are much more stable than pairs and groups. Long-term projects require them. Because associations between the members of these organizations are contractual, impersonal as well as instrumental and, for many, even anonymous, individuals can get a great deal for relatively little effort out of membership in them. The lack of concern for the personal affairs of individuals by corporate authorities is balanced by the fact that the great majority of the people who man corporate organizations is not required to be concerned about the essential problems of corporations either. The contractual nature of the associations between people who constitute the personnel or clients of large organizations requires only that they be responsible for the terms of their contracts.

Therefore, if they have the prescribed prerequisites and if they follow the rules, prescribed benefits are automatically forthcoming, whether these are in the form of a paycheck, medical care, a college diploma, or whatever. These benefits are independent of personal differences such as charm, wealth, family connections, parentage, etc. The acquisition of the prerequisites is the rub that is felt by many without them. No amount of pleading or presentation of a different set of assets will evoke the benefits. Large organizations must be all but impervious to special cases and special pleading if they are to achieve the ends for which they are the most efficient type of organization.

The rigidity of the requirements often becomes irksome to some of the beneficiaries of corporations. Impersonality and depersonalization are resented by almost everyone sometimes, and by some people all the time. They do not realize, or do not recall, that corporations could not function to do what they do if they did treat individuals as personally significant, beyond a very general level of ordinary propriety and general humane responsibility. Personal involvement in large organizations means favoritism, nepotism, the manipulation of the organization for the advantage of few at the expense of many. So, large organizations are never cozy. If coziness is wanted, people must seek groups and pairs. But these organizations do provide valuable resources for very limited involvement by beneficiaries.

This is as true for employees as it is for clients or stockholders. It is as true in corporate schools and church organizations as it is in economic corporations. It is as true in large administrative organizations whether they are political, religious, or philanthropic, or whatever. Extensive individual effort may be necessary to acquire the prerequisites for membership in a corporation, but once in, the division of labor is such that little enough is demanded to stay in it and receive one's pay or other benefits, unless one is an executive or manager or staff member at a fairly high level. Small operations carry little responsibility and eight hours a day with lunch and coffee breaks is all that is asked from most people. It is remarkably easy to make one's living in large organizations, as compared to self-employment of any kind, or to most executive activities, or to employment in groups. Even promotion is all but guaranteed, once one has been accepted. In some large organizations, acceptance is marked by guarantees of "tenure" and "on-going wages" after retirement, in the form of pensions. Some people may be impatient and compete with the people on their levels for promotion and may be moved along a little faster thereby, but those who simply do their daily stint and become more competent and efficient simply by virtue of repetition and experience will also move up the lines, within certain ranges, over time. Success, as registered improvement of one's position in these organizations over years, is often described as a struggle to get up a ladder. For many, once on it, it is more like being on an escalator.

Large organizations are supposed to select personnel and promote them solely on the basis of objective criteria and efficiency and to distribute goods and services to all who meet standard requirements. There are exceptions enough to this to support a cynical conviction held by many individuals that the only way to get along and ahead is to "know the right people." But what most individuals object to when they criticize and resent large organizations is the fact that they cannot elicit special treatment from authorities in them, that these do in fact select and provide on the basis of standard criteria for the most part. Socially immature people, or people who confuse corporate organizations with groups, continue to expect special consideration and count on the magical manipulation or coercion of elders and authorities for obtaining what they want, not on voluntary cultivation and use of their own resources.

Effective membership in large organizations requires additions to the socialization that is an outcome of experience with particular others and groups. Self-regulation and recognition of the intrinsic value of people in general must be highly developed for competent participation in them. Without self-regulation the size of corporate membership that makes constant supervision of each one difficult enables individuals to neglect the activities they contracted to perform. This interferes with the activity of other members and may interfere with the ability of the organization to achieve its goals. Without generalized respect for others, the impersonality and anonymity of the associations in corporations encourages the exploitation of some by those people for whom other people are merely instrumental means to their own ends.

It may be that exposure to corporate settings too early in a life career interferes with the social development of the actually young who have too few direct personal relationships in which they can discover the intrinsic value of others and, therefore, of themselves. In industrial societies young children and juveniles are more frequently subjected to corporate sources for education, recreation, medical care, and so forth, and more and more families are becoming incapable of supplying these. This may be the real basis for the current widespread demands for the reorganization of public schools and "community" control, and the real need for it however this is being exploited by socially immature adults for reasons that have nothing to do with either the education or the socialization of the young. Certainly, some new and particular interpersonal contexts must be added to those that have served in the past if enough young people are to reach the level of social competence that is necessary both for their own maintenance in complex industrial societies and the maintenance of the societies as well. It may be that school services can be organized to these ends. If not, others must be if the socialization of the young is to be adequate for their adult performance in large, industrial societies. Corporate organizations cannot be competent socializing agents for them.

But the fact that large organizations are not suited to provide the conditions needed for the socialization of the chronologically young does not mean that they are unsuitable for other purposes. They are the most efficient organizational technique for the coordination of the activity of many people doing many kinds of things, or for the distribution of goods and services to large numbers of people. Besides, large corporate and administrative organizations are inescapably major units of organization for technically complex societies with large and heterogeneous populations.

Consequently, more people in these societies must be socialized to high levels of self-regulation if they are to achieve their own satisfactions and contribute to the maintenance of the societies themselves. The stability of contractual and impersonal relationships requires it. They must also be led to recognize that large organizations are socially distinct from groups and that they cannot expect the same responses from the personnel of large organizations that they evoke in their family members, teammates, and friends.

In large industrial societies, it is not only relations in the large corporate organizations that are contractual. Residence in these societies is conspicuously urban, the more industrial, the more urban, and the larger the cities in them. It is these societies that have given rise to the metropolis, which is very different from traditional cities. Both civil order in these large urban residential areas and the personal comfort of the individuals in them also depend upon the development of ability to manifest respect for strangers and to act with responsibility to a contract as well as responsibility to particular people in direct exchanges with one another. They have to come to recognize that a contract is, in essence, an indirect commitment to people whose satisfaction depends upon it.

General Conclusions Concerning Socialization and Social Order

By and large, the factors involved in socialization are universal and so are its manifestations. The series of interpersonal contexts that effect it are evoked by the psychobiological necessities of the growing young, for the most part. However, once human beings have acquired the social skills that are chiefly dictated by their own psychobiological needs, it is clear that further socialization may be required for, and evoked by, conditions inherent in complex organization itself rather than in human characteristics and needs.[4] This fact has become apparent in societies on which some of the characteristics of modern, industrial societies have recently been imposed, and in modern, industrial societies themselves, where populations have become more heterogeneous, where the range of culture has become more extensive and technological, and where units of organization have become increasingly large and impersonal. The socialization of individuals that these require, and its effects, are not universal, but they are the same wherever these social conditions arise.

The need for individual adaptation by so many people to social organizations that are not directly connected with individual psychobiological resources is a new phenomenon. People are dependent for the satisfaction of many of their basic needs on these interpersonal arrangements, but the social constraints on their biological impulses to attain them not only are great, but are separated from particular people. The members of large organizations are continuously shifted and replaced. The adaptation to others and techniques for manipulating them that are acquired in groups in which people are in direct reciprocities are of no avail in dealing with large organizations. No one person is responsible for another's welfare, or even, in most instances, for the whole of the service sought. Therefore, there is no particular one to respond to. Unless people are highly cultivated, there are no stimuli to initiate the self-regulated social restraints that they exercise toward particular others.

The nature of large organizations can only be grasped conceptually. Large organizations cannot be encountered in toto directly. The relation of their many parts, only some of which are known to each person involved in them, to their products and services, is complicated. It is not surprising that the immature of all ages, and the uneducated, do not either use or man large organizations efficiently, or to

[4] The problems of human adaptation to large, industrial societies are thoughtfully considered by Robert Nisbet, *The Quest for Community* (New York: Oxford University Press, 1953); *The Sociological Tradition* (New York: Basic Books, 1956).

their own satisfaction. There is too much about large organizations that is not only impersonal, but abstract.

This is why I do not think that they are suitable organizations for undertaking any task that demands personal attention and direct experience for its achievement. This includes such things as educating the young, welfare services, medical care, the care of the old, and so forth. In my opinion, much of the current student turmoil stems from the fact that so many schools, especially public schools, have become corporate organizations. The young not only want individual attention, but need it. Denied it, they do what all children do when frustrated, they withdraw cooperation from the elders who seem to be failing them and revert to the more violent tactics in their repertoires of possible responses to others to command attention. The nature of their demands shows little understanding either of their own basic needs or of the nature of organizations, but what they do indicates both their need for peers and, being juvenile and adolescent, for the most part, they disclose their need for information and cultivation by their elders by compelling them to pay attention to them. Like juveniles and adolescents of all ages, they all believe they are more autonomous and devoted to one another than they are. They have a very limited understanding of what they need to acquire for their future competence and well-being. But they seem to be aware that the large organizations that their schools have become are not giving it to them, and, in ways they often do not understand, they are right. Rebellious welfare clients and the neglected and miserable sick and old are further testimony that large organizations are unsuitable for personal services to the socially immature or handicapped.

However, when the socially immature and handicapped denounce all large organizations they are displaying ignorance. Many of their satisfactions are made available by large organizations. In any case, technically elaborate societies cannot exist without them. Therefore, the people who live in them must be socialized to do so. Just as the negotiation of the resources of childhood is essential for the realization of the resources of the juvenile phase, or of the juvenile for pre-adolescence, and so forth, so the social skills of young adults are needed as a base for adaptation to acting effectively as a social unit in large organizations. Once this is achieved, training programs in these organizations can develop the social techniques for operating in them, if the people who run them are aware that this requires some cultivation of their inexperienced personnel. Currently, most of them do. In-service training is widespread in corporations. They are less likely to recognize the unsuitability of large organizations for some purposes.

In large industrial societies, the socialization that follows mainly from the interpersonal contexts that human psychobiological attributes themselves evoke are still necessary; they are only insufficient. Something new has been added. The characteristics of large organizations are chiefly the outcome of the large numbers of people involved, not their individual psychobiological characteristics, and the large numbers of them are required for technical reasons. The cultivation of social ability for acting as social units in them requires much greater limitation on individual psychobiological impulses than living in groups does and, unlike most groups, their connection with individual satisfactions is very indirect for most participants. As a result, few individuals are likely to acquire the skills that these organizations need unless they are subject to a great many coercions to do so.

Some of these are already apparent. If large organizations are the only source of the means to satisfy basic needs, people begin to adapt to them. If their maintenance becomes associated with the maintenance of their society, people begin to support them. If they supply occupational training and, especially, if they supply professional training, membership in them can even take on the quality of membership called primary. But this is only possible for individuals who have reached the juvenile level of social development at least, and it increasingly depends upon extensive education as well. The abstract aspects of large organizations as well as the technology they employ make competent literacy an absolute requisite for participation in them. As a result of the increase in the number of people who are either members or clients of large organizations, more and more individuals in the complex societies that give rise to them are being socialized to operate in them.

This is achieved in part by much the same techniques that are employed to cultivate individuals to be effective units in families and peer-groups. Insofar as large organizations are sources of satisfaction—income and opportunity to cultivate and exercise ability being their most common benefit to personnel, and goods and services for clients—the people who run them have the most basic of all coercions at their command, namely, control of access to what individuals need and want. Clearly formulated systems of approval and disapproval and of reward and punishment are highly developed in large organizations.

The basic organizational units of these organizations are groups and a distinct hierarchy of administrators and executives. The coercions of reward and punishment operate much as they do for juvenile peer-groups. Each group unit, usually a department, is roughly a peer-group in terms of some particular skills or knowledge, cooperating to reach a common goal, directed by a "head," who is roughly the equivalent of the "team captain." Individuals communicate directly with their department-mates and their "head." He mediates between them and administrators. Administrators communicate directly with executives. The latter determine the tasks, the benefits and their distribution for the organization as a whole, but only the part of this that is relevant to each group routinely reaches it. Like team members, members of the units of large organizations know both the activities and the requirements for participation in them before they join them. Once in them, like team members, ultimate authority is remote for most of them and reaches them directly only in exceptional circumstances. Routinely, the approvals and disapprovals of their immediate department mates, even their power of ostracism from the informal exchanges between them, and the authority of their own head serve to coerce those individuals who need coercion. If that does not work, the administrators and/or executives call them to account directly and they, unlike family elders, have the ultimate power to exclude an offending member from the organization.

No actual organization runs as smoothly as this. There are always "personnel problems," which means that individual and personal factors do arise in large organizations, and which also reveals that personal factors frequently do not contribute to the maintenance of large organizations and often interfere with their functions. Still, in a general way, large organizations are run in part as a series of teams, held together by a series of overlapping memberships in administrative and executive groups. This is why people with juvenile social skills can operate efficiently in large organizations.

But these group units are not true juvenile peer-groups. Their activities are not completed by them, they are partial contributions to ends that very often are unknown to department members. These have not come together out of the need for peers, and, strictly speaking, they are members of the large organization, not of their groups. Actual juvenile peer-groups are much more impersonal than juveniles recognize, but the group units of large organizations are even more impersonal. Informality must not be confused with actual concern for others. As is the case with juveniles, some particular people may come to have direct personal significance in these groups. If so, this is tolerated even less in the group units of large organizations than in true juvenile peer-groups. Friendships are viewed with suspicion as a source of favoritism and family relationships are usually forbidden in recruitment. Marriage is often reason for dismissal. Furthermore, because the activities of these unit groups are only partial contributions to much larger purposes, they have to be highly standardized and more attention must be paid to what other groups are doing than is the case for true juvenile groups. It is ideally desirable for each person to feel that his essential responsibility is to the whole organization and its ultimate goals. It is essential that some of them do so.

This responsibility to the whole is what is beyond the capacities of socially juvenile adults. Childish ones are utterly incompetent in these social settings. No juvenile of any age will be constrained on behalf of people he does not know and activities that make no visible contribution to his own interests, unless effective coercions are apparent to him. So, the maintenance of large organizations requires more socialization than the juvenile level represents in a considerable proportion of its members, especially in its administrators and executives. This is chiefly cultivated in those who do not bring these abilities with them by a variety of in-service training programs. Their appeal has to be made to the minds of the personnel, for the most part, and herein lies a difficulty. A relatively high level of conceptual development becomes a requisite for effective and satisfying participation in large organizations. The requirements and the nature of the cultivation, and the final social modification of the individuals that marks their socialization for this kind of membership, is very like those for the cultivation of professional people. In fact, just as individuals become doctors or lawyers, some people are transformed into "organization men,"[5] and women as well.

Critics of this development are likely to be Cassandras crying in the wilderness for at least as long as technology is advanced at its present rates. If elaborate technical arrangements are desired, large organizations are inevitable. They are probably reacting to the increased restraints on individual impulses which they recognize these organizations impose on those who participate in them. They have overlooked the fact that for those who have the social competence to operate comfortably in them, these organizations provide considerable benefit for relatively little individual effort and leave them freer to pursue more personal satisfactions than participation in pairs and primary groups do. They have not suggested how the extraordinary capacity of large organizations for production of goods and services can be achieved without them. Finally, they have not mentioned the fact that, at least for the foreseeable future, people who want to avoid these organizations can do so as long as they are also willing to do without the benefits they provide. In any case, socialization will be extended for an increasing number of people to enable them to benefit from and participate in these organizations and to live in the kind of residential areas that become characteristic for

[5] William H. Whyte, Jr., *Organization Man* (New York: Simon and Schuster, 1956). Excellent description of this process.

them as well. Those who acquire this social skill are and will be as unaware of the complex factors, coercions, and effort that went into this accomplishment as all people are of any of the individual modifications that are an outcome of their socialization, of whatever kind.

In essence, socialization is independent of particular cultural requirements, being adaptations and developments evoked by the presence of people and organizations, whatever their culture. The relationships necessary for individual human survival, development and maintenance, those that are often called "significant others" and "primary groups" are more the same for all human beings than not, regardless of their cultural elaborations. Mothering, family groups, play groups, relations with peers and the opposite sex, are all associations evoked by psychobiological needs and capacities; they are made only more complex and elaborate by cultural prescriptions. The interpersonal contexts that characterize complex societies and the social skills they require and cultivate are similar wherever they occur also because forms of organization have their own inherent requirements.

It is socialization that enables individuals to live among people of different cultures. If socialization were essentially culturally determined, people could not travel from one society to another in a different cultural area. When people speak of the "human condition" which binds them to one another because they share the same basic necessities and the same essential relationships, they are referring to the factors that determine their socialization, not their cultural ingredients. If they can conceive of this common humanity it is because they are extensively socialized. Infants and children feel unique because they are imprisoned by their somatic impulses; juveniles, because they experience their cultural means as universal and absolute. Psychobiology and socialization are what socially mature people have in common. The two strongly influence each other.

The pioneer work on socialization was overwhelmingly focused on child-development and the bulk of the literature still is. Freud included infancy and childhood and the juvenile era, and early studies of so-called juvenile delinquency extended it to include adolescence. As a consequence of this history, the notion still generally prevails that the processes involved in socialization begin at birth and continue to some ill-defined stage of development called "social maturity" roughly associated with biological maturity, but not necessarily so. In the Freudian view, for example, it is assumed that basic patterns for important relationships are fixed even before biological adolescence. For others, adolescence is the final determining phase. In general, the adage "you can't teach an old dog new tricks" describes the assumptions of a good many students of socialization and this implies that the processes available for social development are exhausted at some point in the life span. It also overlooks the fact that human beings are not "dogs" and have potential resources that greatly exceed those of "man's best friend."

It is true that by the time people are biologically adult the fate of many of their potentialities have been largely determined. Some skills have been cultivated and not others. The relationships and organizations that provide an individual with satisfactions and security have been imposed or selected and are relatively stable. Occupations and mates have been chosen. Children have been born. In short, as we proceed in our life-careers our degrees of freedom for choosing what we might, or might not be or do, narrow. The range is never much wider than the relationships that are within the reach of the people with whom we are actually in contact, originally directly, and subsequently by means of mediated communications. And so, in some respects, some changes in biologically adult people become impossible and the rates of change slow down and the range of probable change narrows.

However, both psychobiological processes and adaptations to other people do continue throughout the life-span. They also change. The relationships that sustain an individual are modified or cease to exist. New ones are established. Sometimes individuals even acquire particular significant relationships for the first time rather late in life, a heterosexual relationship, or a friend, for example, and thereby achieve a stage of social development that they missed at the time that many of their contemporaries negotiated it. Loss of social competence is more common, especially by the sick and old.

Conspicuous new socialization in adults is most often associated with dramatic shifts in their total social situation that result from such events as immigration, war, entrance into the armed forces, or a religious order. But whether or not people are confronted with exceptional life circumstances, the life-span of each person involves continuous changes that require the same kinds of adaptation of their resources to people that are required in early life. Every decade or so the hierarchy of human needs shifts for individuals as physical resources wax and wane, mental resources expand and contract, the people long relied upon scatter and die, and relations with those who remain change by virtue of additional years, if nothing else. To all such inescapable changes, each human being must adapt if he is to maintain his own level of social development, satisfy his needs, and contribute to the social organizations that supply him with what he needs and wants. It is this kind of adaptation that constitutes socialization and it continues throughout the human life span.

Chapter Nine

Some General Connections between Individual Social Development and Social Organizations: Enculturation

ENCULTURATION is the term that I use to refer to the second major category of factors and the resources and the conditions for their cultivation, that, in combination with *socialization*, constitute the social development of individuals. This term was introduced into social science by anthropologists and, by and large, my use of it is the same as theirs. I differ from them in maintaining a much stricter differentiation of *enculturation* from *socialization* than most of them do. Also I do not subscribe to their use of *acculturation* to refer to the *enculturation* of adults, immigrants, for example, because in my opinion the processes and conditions involved, and their results, are essentially the same throughout the life-cycle of human beings.

I use the word *enculturation* to refer to all the factors and processes that lead to the acquisition by individuals of a repertoire of cultural entities—consensually validated words, concepts, meanings, systematic knowledge, skills, etc.—as an integral part of their apparatus for language performance, mental activities, and many functions of their biological systems. Obviously, enculturation cannot take place in the absence of other people, and so it proceeds along with socialization, but it is primarily a development in response to their transmission of culture, not to them as

192

persons. After the early years of life, and if the higher mental functions have been developed, enculturation can be forwarded by means of mediated sources: books, records, pictures, etc. Since all cultural entities are products of collective human life they are essentially independent of particular people and so the enculturation of individuals ultimately transcends necessity for personal adaptations to the other people who have fostered it. It is more closely related to the fact that culture is a product of human mental activity than to the nature of human interdependence for the satisfaction of on-going maintenance needs.

Enculturation is very closely related to the most unique characteristic of human beings, namely, their particular kind of mental operations. Adult human beings use symbols and meanings as their principal means for organizing experience. Without this ability, human organizations and institutions would be impossible. Yet this vital function is not guaranteed by the human equipment involved in it: the human brain, central nervous system, and apparatus for speech. The somatic growth of these structures produces none of the more complex human mental functions. In this respect, these structures differ from the other vital systems of the human body. Even the long-delayed and complex capacity for reproduction is released by growth alone.

But the mental functions which distinguish human beings from other living creatures, and on which all human social life depends, require that a language and a repertoire of validated symbols and meanings, *et al.*, be stably integrated into the physical structures which make them possible before these can perform their functions. How this occurs we still do not know and our ignorance is a great impediment to the advancement of social science. But we do know that it occurs, that it is necessary both for individual psychobiological and social development to maturity and the maintenance of collective arrangements for human living. We know some of the conditions that promote it. We know some of the consequences of failure to achieve it.

We also know that this development in mankind involves liabilities as well as assets. Harry Stack Sullivan used to point out that although the human ability for the creation and use of symbols accounts for man's greatest adaptations, it also accounts for his greatest maladaptations. It is the basis for creative talent. It also makes psychosis possible. Recently, Konrad Lorenz commented on this problem as it affects mankind collectively:

> It is a curious paradox that the greatest gifts of man, the unique faculties of conceptual thought and verbal speech which have raised him to a level high above all other creatures and given him mastery over the globe, are not altogether blessings, or at least, are blessings that have to be paid for very dearly indeed. All the great dangers threatening humanity with extinction are direct consequences of conceptual thought and verbal speech. Knowledge springing from conceptual thought robbed man of the security provided by his well-adapted instincts long, long before it was sufficient to provide him with an equally safe adaptation.[1]

In evolutionary terms, our mental functions and consequent dependence on enculturation for adult competence are new. It may be that evolutionary processes will select for conceptual capacity among us and provide biological changes that will make its development in each one of us less problematic than it now is. Meanwhile, however, we are in danger of destroying ourselves with it. By making collective human life more and more dependent upon cultural invention, transmission and use, these mental activities have made it uncomfortably insecure. At the same time, inequality of access to adaptive cultural resources is becoming a threat to survival for both human individuals and human populations.

The necessary transmission of a repertoire of symbols and meanings to each human individual by the elders upon whom they are dependent for survival and development, and their stable integration of it, is a major part of what I refer to when I use the word *enculturation*. But this is not all that it refers to. In the course of supplying the means to all the organic needs that dominate the human young, their elders elaborate access to those satisfactions and the satisfactions themselves by cultural additions. The timing of at-

---

[1] Konrad Lorenz, *On Aggression* (New York: Harcourt Brace, 1963), p. 238.

tention, the amount and the particular kind of food, clothing, shelter, etc., the conditions for achieving sexual satisfaction, and so on, are determined by the cultural traits of the people who tend the young. And so, from birth, the line between felt organic need and its satisfaction is not a direct one for human beings. It is not simply determined by biological need and the presence in the environment of the means to assuage it. It is elongated and made increasingly complex by the cultural conditions imposed by the people who control access to the means of satisfaction.

Since these cultural additions are interferences with access to biological satisfactions and make for a more complicated way of life, the young do not cry for them. Their organisms neither impel them to seek these modifications nor provide clues to what they are. Only the power of their elders to coerce them leads the human young to acquire the cultural resources they need for their own development and for their ability as adults to attain satisfactions by their own efforts. In time, these induced modifications of organized functions come to be experienced as "natural." There is little or no awareness of how they came into existence, or that it took tedious repetition of persuasion and coercion on the part of many others to establish what we have come to experience as our most private and treasured beliefs, values, tastes, etc. The conviction of most people that their language is as inherent a part of them as their fingers and toes, and the only one that really makes sense, is only one of many examples of the fact that we are scarcely aware that our personal traits are so dependent upon the people and culture available to us. All of this is also enculturation and most of it works as automatically, once it has been cultivated, as organic processes.

It should be obvious that the word *learning* in its ordinary sense is not adequate to cover this cluster of human phenomena. Such phrases as "the internalization of the norms" or "the incorporation of parental images" do not describe it either. The outcome of the evolutionary developments in human beings that eventuated in their creation of symbols for organizing experience and of their use of language for communication also eventuated in their creation and accumulation of the realm of phenomena we call "culture." Apparently, the more of this that mankind created and accumulated, the more dependent mankind became upon its creation and use for its own development and maintenance. In essence, all cultural entities represent a kind of coding of human experience and knowledge into languages, tools, concepts, skills, and combinations thereof, into elaborate systems of knowledge, customs, beliefs, rules, ideals, art, literature, and so on.

By use of these, human beings freed themselves from the limits of immediacy and space that so circumscribe the lives of all other animals and became able to modify progressively the physical and organic realms to suit their own ends. What is more, they became capable of modifying themselves to an extraordinary degree, though conceivably not enough as yet, and of dominating some of their biological impulses by conceptual interference with them, which is what we refer to as self-regulation. In other words, within limits, human beings could restrain organic impulses to immediate satisfactions and thus escape the repetitive patterns of hunting, eating, sleeping, mating, and procreating in fixed sequences that dominate other animals. More complicated ways of life became open to them, perhaps too complicated.

Cultural entities are never the outcome of individual abilities for symbol making and use alone. They only emerge out of communication between human beings. Any individual innovation must be recognized and conceptually grasped by other human beings and formulated into communicable symbols before it becomes part of culture. It is in this way that the experiences and conceptions of individuals have become a vast resource for the whole of mankind. But it is also true that each individual has the capacity to acquire and decode symbols and, within limits, to use them to regulate his behavior and increase his competence even without direct experience of their referents, that culture persists and is an ingredient of all human behavior and social phenomena.

Thus, although culture is a product of collective life, it is never independent of individual human abilities for acquiring and using it and individual enculturation. Culture, in itself, does nothing, though we are often told that it does. It neither creates, nor preserves, nor transmits itself. It does not even impose itself on human beings, only other human beings do that. It is not culture that resists change, but the nature of the enculturation of human individuals.

The chief manifestations of enculturation are the human use of language, the modifications of human organic structures and functions that result from the integration of the cultural entities imposed by elders on the young, or authorities on the older, the conceptual content of what are called "minds," and a category of wants, as distinct from psychobiological maintenance needs, which are originally defined by significant other people in their cultural terms and imposed as conditions for access to satisfactions. Considering the fact that none of this is specifically determined by the psychobiological potential for it, it is amazing that it comes to be experienced by the people in whom it is cultivated as though it were inherent in their organisms. The satisfaction of culturally defined wants that are an outcome of initial coercions by others often takes precedence in human adults over the satisfaction of somatic needs, even when this threatens survival. Thousands of human beings have died in defense of ideas, of honor, or of political and religious doctrines.

However, this remarkable cultural modification of human organisms and, hence, of stable culturally determined behavior by human adults, only operates smoothly as long as it is unwitting. Harry Stack Sullivan suggested that:

> The vast rote-learning of culture is the general instance of which sublimation as seen in psychiatry is a special instance by which the victim, without knowing it, finds a socially acceptable way of living. It satisfies more or less something given, but it follows socially approved patterns. The operational attack on sublimation is that if you tell people how they can sublimate they can't sublimate. In other words, the unwitting part of it—the fact that it is not run through consciousness—is what makes it work.[2]

[2] H. S. Sullivan, "Illusion of Personal Individuality," in *Psychiatry*, Vol. VIII, No. 3, pp. 323-324.

And William Sumner noted before Sullivan that "thought is the worst enemy of the mores."[3]

Sociologists have not only failed to clearly distinguish between socialization and enculturation, but have tended to see the enculturation of individuals only in what they call the "internalization of norms and values," and the "learning of roles." These are, indeed, an important part of enculturation. They constitute the beliefs and ethics and standards of propriety and skills and rituals that particular populations share because the people who reared and cultivated them transmitted these, and not other ones, and that other populations do not share, because their elders used other norms and values and roles to standardize individual behavior. Sociologists are especially concerned with the organization of people into collective units and the cultural means to this end have to be standardized to accomplish it. This focus on requirements for organization has led sociologists to underestimate the profundity of the changes wrought in individuals by their acquisition of these cultural items. They have also tended to confuse what more properly belongs to "formal learning" with the integration of culture as part of the structure and function of psychobiological equipment. Consequently, they have overlooked the many other aspects of enculturation and their relation to the ability of individuals to operate as effective social units in organizations.

Enculturation has particular sociological significance because the traits that are cultivated in the process are precisely the ones that identify individuals as members of particular organizations. Socialization is important to sociological analysis because it develops ability for maintaining stable relationships in a variety of interpersonal arrangements, *per se*. But socialization in itself does not equip people to operate in particular organizations, only in types of relationship and organization. Enculturation is necessary for particular memberships. A particular language, particular values, particular norms, particular skills, or particular knowledge is required for membership in every particular

[3] William Graham Sumner, *Folkways* (New York: Mentor Books, 1962).

social organization. Unlike the skills represented by stages of socialization, one language is not useful among people who speak another. The most extensive enculturation for becoming a lawyer cannot be used to become a doctor. Even the most highly enculturated members of one society are gravely disadvantaged in another until they are enculturated with the language, norms, and so forth, of the new one. The social skills developed in socialization are transferable, most of those that are an outcome of enculturation are not. Only the fact that all human beings are enculturated is universal.

Enculturation not only differentiates the population of one society from another, but differentiates categories within populations and members of different organizations. Unless individuals are socialized enough to recognize the intrinsic nature of human beings, and many adults are not, they identify people as persons like themselves by their enculturation, not by their general human traits or levels of socialization. Therefore, for people who are capable of forming stable relationships only with people like themselves, it is enculturation that determines the relationships they can tolerate. According to the old adage, "Birds of a feather flock together." For human beings it is enculturation that is the plumage that determines friends and enemies. It may be worth noting that differences in plumage distinguish male from female and young from old birds as well. This is the basis of chauvinism, ethnocentrism, religious animosities, and snobbery. Because what has been enculturated has been integrated into the apparatus that regulates each individual's behavior, and regulates most of it automatically, the sorting of people on the basis of their enculturation is perpetuated by their self-regulation.

Enculturation is probably the greatest impediment to significant social change that is not unwitting or so gradual that the changes induced at any given time do not run counter to established practice. Even what are usually called "vested interests" generally involve impulses to obtain or retain something that contributes to essential biological satisfactions, or the means to them. They can be changed easily enough if the individuals involved can see their way to these satisfactions in the proposed arrangement. It is not the pursuit of "food, clothing, and shelter," and other sensual satisfactions that has to be cultivated by coercions on the part of elders. On the contrary, it is the limitation of these pursuits and insistence on their cultural elaborations that have to be imposed.

Because enculturation always interferes with direct satisfaction of needs, it is enculturation that requires the application of a battery of coercions, the most important of which is the deliberate evocation of anxiety. Unless a cultural taboo accompanied by threats of dire consequences has been attached to the eating of foods, people have little difficulty in acquiring new food habits. Pork is made inedible to Jews and Moslems by enculturation, but they have no problem eating local vegetables in a strange land. Failure to conform to an anxiety-enforced cultural item in one's repertoire arouses such apprehension that few people risk so doing if they can avoid it.

The fact that the apprehension and embarrassment and shame evoked by cultural non-conformity are all derivatives of anxiety, the source of which is unknown or unrecognized by the victims, and that the consequences threatened are vague and unverified, makes it extremely unlikely that most people will embrace it voluntarily. If a deliberate attempt is made to impose it upon them, they will resist it with every means at their disposal. This is what is behind Sumner's dictum that one "cannot legislate against the mores."[4] The folkways and mores of any population are an important part of what is transmitted to their young as enculturation. That these define their individual tastes, beliefs, convictions, opinions, *et al*, and that they will even die for, or kill others for some of them, under the impression that they are acting as unique individuals, is a measure of the fundamental modifications of psychobiological resources that enculturation induces. They cannot be changed easily. Some cannot be changed at all in particular individuals.

Culture and enculturation have greatly augmented human potentialities and human life, indeed, peculiarly human life is inconceivable without them. They are the most powerful

[4] *Ibid.*

means human beings have for maintaining themselves. Nevertheless, like the capacity for conceptual thought on which they depend, the creation and use of culture by human beings have introduced serious hazards to both individuals and their collective arrangements.

Although enculturation unites people who share it, it is probably the greatest source of divisiveness and enmity between people who do not. In the modern world, people no longer eliminate one another in pursuit of biological satisfactions nearly as often as they eliminate one another for cultural reasons. This is why direct application of the concept of "territoriality" as this is manifest in other animals to human beings is inappropriate.[5] It is probable that the technology that makes it possible for some people to produce much more than they need for their own maintenance and that has created means for distributing surplus has contributed to further loosening the ties that bind other animals to particular localities for mankind.

In any case, major conflicts in the contemporary world are in defense of culture areas, or are attempts to impose particular cultural practices on populations, not for territory itself. Furthermore, because only culture in general, and not particular cultural phenomena, is universal for the species of man, unlike the factors that apparently evoke territorial defenses in other animals, cultural boundaries that might guarantee non-aggression within their limits and serve as effective restraints on people of different culture are fluctuating and unstable. Culture is not even distributed evenly within populations. It is possible that innate animal aggression in defense of territory in man has been detached from real estate and transferred to culture, but if so, the ritual defenses and protections that keep peace between animals have not been devised.

Just as we must be careful to avoid anthropomorphism—regarding animals as people—so, however much we may learn that is suggestive and instructive by studying animal behavior, we must be careful how we apply these lessons when we interpret human behavior. For man is certainly an animal, but man, al-

[5] Robert Ardrey, *The Territorial Imperative* (New York: Dell, 1966).

though identifiably a primate, is also a primate of a unique—and uniquely dangerous—species.[6]

The substitution of culture, transmitted as enculturation, for genetically transmitted means for the regulation of human behavior and collective order, has introduced an element of great uncertainty and divisiveness into human life. Cultural formulations and prescriptions and devices are always based on the past experience of human beings. Important changes in the physical or social conditions for their living may make particular cultural items obsolete, unuseful, even fatal, for both individuals and populations. Yet, there are no guarantees that suitable cultural means will be created to meet the new circumstances. Necessity may be the mother of invention, but it may be barren. Anxiety-enforced enculturation may cause people to persist on a lethal course.

Despite these hazards, human beings have no choice with respect to the creation and use of culture, Rousseauian and other notions of culturally unfettered, "natural" men notwithstanding.

> Man is by nature a being of culture. Man's whole system of innate activities and reactions is phylogenetically so constructed as to need to be complemented by cultural tradition. For instance, all the tremendous neuro-sensory apparatus of human speech is phylogenetically evolved but so constructed that its function presupposes the existence of a culturally developed language which the infant has to learn. The greater part of all phylogenetically evolved patterns of human social behavior is interrelated with cultural tradition in an analogous way. The urge to become a member of a group is certainly something that has been programmed in the pre-human phylology of man, but the distinctive properties of any group are norms ritualized in cultural development.[7]
>
> Norms of social behavior developed by cultural ritualization play at least as important a part in the context of human society as instinctive motivation ... customs and taboos may

[6] Konrad Lorenz in an article by Joseph Alsop in *The New Yorker* (March 8, 1969), p. 88.

[7] Lorenz, *On Aggression, op. cit.*, p. 265.

acquire the power to motivate behavior in a way comparable to that of autonomous instincts.[8]

> Were it possible to rear a human being without culture the result would not be a reconstruction of a pre-human ancestor, as yet devoid of culture. It would be a poor cripple deficient in higher functions. ... No man, not even the greatest genius, could invent all by himself a system of social norms and rites forming a substitute cultural tradition.[9]

The transformation of the psychobiological potentialities of young human organisms into manifest adult skills for living among others and maintaining themselves requires the extensive enculturation of the organic structures and functions of each of them, especially of those associated with linguistic and mental competence. Similar enculturation is one of the strongest ties between people. It is the mark of common memberships. It is similar enculturation, not biological traits, that transforms a population into a people. Yet, the cultural items involved in the enculturation of everyone are not always useful and may even be destructive, and important differences in enculturation are as potent barriers to associations between human beings as shared enculturation is a spur to their unions.

In contrast to socialization, which may be insufficient in particular individuals, but which always promotes stable relationships between people, enculturation introduces potential dangers into the life of human beings that are inherent in the kind of creatures they are. These dangers cannot be eliminated, but conceivably they can be avoided in some measure if people are made aware of them. The way out of the essentially unwitting regulation of behavior that is determined by enculturation is the use of rational mental processes.

[8] *Ibid.*, p. 258.

[9] *Ibid.*, p. 265.

Chapter Ten

The Mental Foundation of
Human Social Life

THE SOCIAL DEVELOPMENT of human beings, and the consequences of it, depend, in the final analysis, on human mental capacities. George Mead's recognition that the connection between "self" and "society" is "mind" was a seminal insight.[1] Ignorance of the nature of "mind" remains a handicap to the understanding of social phenomena, but we do have some information about what it does and one thing we know is that it operates on different levels of awareness, with different results. A great deal of socialization and enculturation occurs outside the awareness of the people undergoing them, and often outside the awareness of the people who induce them, as well as by means of deliberate conceptual thought. Different effects follow from the different levels of awareness involved.

The socialization and enculturation that by-pass conscious conceptual effort result in conditioning and imprinting. Conditioning, in the Pavlovian sense, refers to the modification or augmentation of any pattern of behavior by its subjection to the repetition of new conditions until they come to be automatically associated with the initial sequence. The dog that salivated to the sound of a bell as well as to the sight and smell of food is the classical example. Imprinting refers to the fact that:

> There are certain patterns of behavior that are fully innate as patterns but are not hooked up onto a releasing mechanism, as it were, until a young bird or animal has passed through a critical—and measurable—stage of growth.[2]

[1] George Mead, *Mind, Self and Society* (Chicago: University of Chicago Press, 1946).

[2] Lorenz, *op. cit. The New Yorker.* p. 58.

The "hook-up" at the appropriate time is "imprinting." It is clearly involved in the initiation of speech and language performance in human beings, in the cultivation of conceptual abilities, in human sexual performances, and much else.

Much conditioning and imprinting of human beings are achieved by means of rote-learning from and emulation of elders or authorities. They result in a large repertoire of automatic performances. It is chiefly by conditioning and imprinting that the folkways and mores espoused by the people among whom an individual lives become his individual habits, values, attitudes, etc. Because the particular cultural additions to psychobiological structures and functions are not universal, they are not only a mark of particular memberships, but many of them are useless in other or greatly changed social contexts. Because conditioning and imprinting by-passes awareness and thought, the behavior they induce is automatic and is experienced as natural. It is extremely resistant to change.

A very great part of the life of everyone is lived on this level. Modes of eating, sleeping, cleanliness, etc., means to education, religious worship, earning a living, and the maintenance of relations to others, of norms, of taste, manners, and beliefs, and much more, have been established in people in ways that involved no deliberate thought. Individuals do not recall that they acquired them from others or are aware of the countless acts of coercion by others used to establish them as their personal attributes. So long as they lead to a reasonable amount of security and satisfaction and, sometimes, even if they do not, and as long as the people who manifest them do not attempt to live with people whose conditioning and imprinting are significantly different, the regulation of behavior in these ways remains stable, unquestioned, hardly distinguishable by people from their physiological processes. This stabilization of behavior in individuals in a population is a major source of stability for its collective order.

Conditioning and imprinting determine a good many aspects of socialization as well as enculturation. One of the important contributions of Freud, and the psychiatrists and psychologists who have come after him, is the disclosure that the relation between infants and children and the people who take care of them is conditioned and/or imprinted as a basic pattern of what they can expect at the hands of significant other people, and that this conditioning and/or imprinting automatically colors subsequent and different relationships. Freud and Freudians have rather overemphasized family relationships, especially those with parents and siblings. No doubt these influence subsequent relationships, but, in my opinion, the young have other "significant relationships," some of them concomitantly, and for human beings, these are as necessary to release some of their potentialities as family relationships are.

Family relationships are augmented by other elders, such as teachers, doctors, and so on, by peers and friends, and, for that matter, by experience in a variety of organizations, not merely life in a family group. But there is ample evidence that, whatever the nature of the source of imprinting and conditioning, the initial quality of the relationships involved is often projected on to subsequent relationships that in any way recall them.

To the extent that this occurs without awareness or thought, individuals tend to respond to others in particular relationships throughout their lives much as they did to the ones who conditioned and imprinted them in the first place. So much agrees with the contentions of psychoanalysts. But, since adult competence in human beings requires socialization to people in a number of significant relationships other than family relationships, lack of experience with, or adaptation to, them as well as early imprinting can result in lack of social maturity. Adults who respond to all people in authority over them as though they were parents, and to all peers as though they were siblings, can be suffering from social deprivation or pathology as well as psychiatric pathology, or both.

However, the potentiality for abstract conceptualization and systematic thought is innate in all but defective human beings and once their mental capacities are transformed into abilities for conceptualization and thought processes, human beings can transcend mere conditioning and imprinting. They can break up automatic performances, create new modes of behavior, can add new means to satisfaction and security, and acquire alternative patterns of behavior communicated by other people, both directly and indirectly. They can expand their consciousness or awareness of people and things and events far beyond the limits of immediate experience. Among the items of which they become aware are themselves as objects as well as subjects, and other people as subjects as well as objects. Both can become subjects of thought and meaning that transcend mere existence.

This extension of human life gives rise to deliberate invention, improvisation, choice, and foresight as well as to memory and automatic recall. The results of conditioning, emulation, and rote-learning are not recorded in the mode of thought. They are evoked by signals and operate in sets of responses that often become ineffective if attention and thought intervene. For example, walking, breathing, athletic skills, and so forth must be thoughtless for top performance. Anything, injury or sudden admonition from a bystander, that calls attention to activities of this kind, interferes with them. If the recitation by people of a rote-learned poem or speech, or the playing of a rote-learned musical composition are interrupted, they have to "go back" to some point or begin again. However, in varying degrees, human beings store some experience in conceptual constructs, in ways as yet little understood. The processes of thought depend upon selective recall from this store. It is by these complex functions that immediate experience can be attended, analyzed, changed, and transcended. It is by means of these functions that deliberate planned action can be taken. It is by these that human beings achieve a large, abstract realm of experience. The "senses" are augmented by "conceptual sense": meaning, based upon logic, progressions of thought, inferences, deductions, etc.

Once these abilities are available to the young, around the end of the juvenile era, chronologically speaking, the people who socialize and enculturate them use these resources to advance their social development. This approach to socialization and enculturation is usually initiated by what is called "formal" education. It is deliberately exercised and one of its goals is to evoke and maintain attention to the subjects taught. Thought about them is encouraged. Over time, some of what is learned in this way about both relationships and cultural phenomena becomes part of the repertoire of the people taught that governs their behavior more automatically than not. To the extent that it does, their socialization and enculturation are augmented.

A conspicuous example of socialization and enculturation by means of conceptual formulation in clear awareness is the transformation of students into professional people. If they are to become competent, a large proportion of the knowledge, the conceptual tools, and other skills, and the patterns of behavior toward other people that are relevant to their professions must become more automatic than not. The same transformations apply to artists, or workmen, or drivers of cars or planes, or immigrants, indeed to everyone, insofar as repetition and mastery of information or skills which they learned by deliberate conceptual effort becomes part of their automatic equipment. Until this happens, their performance in their special fields remains unreliable. Who trusts a doctor who examines him with a textbook in hand?

Because this level of formulation and skill initially depended upon deliberate thought, it transcends folkways, mores, and traditional lore. It need not be local. To the extent that its acquisition is separated from gross manipulations of means to satisfactions for maintenance, it is apt to escape extensive anxiety-enforcement. Therefore, it remains more readily open to thought, to analysis, to correction, to augmentation whenever something that does not coincide with expectations evokes attention. In this regard, this kind of socialization and enculturation differs from that which occurs on the sub-conceptual level, most of which is associated with anxiety-producing coercions. It is social development that is initiated within awareness that greatly expands adaptability to new conditions and, therefore, an expanded range of living capacity.

All formal learning does not result in the socialization and enculturation of people. In general, enculturation is more amenable to conceptual approaches than socialization. But only a fraction of the cultural resources presented in deliberate learning situations becomes integrated into the apparatus for thought that more or less automatically regulates the behavior of the students, or into their neural and muscular and skeletal apparatus in a way that establishes patterns of motion that work with precision. The myriad skills and information that individuals learn temporarily, usually for specific purposes, such as passing examinations or filling temporary jobs, are not part of their enculturation. They vanish when demand for them ceases. A conspicuous example of socialization by conceptual formulation is provided by successful psychotherapy. This is one of its major goals and it is quite deliberately undertaken. Most of the impersonal relationships that adults in industrial societies establish for various periods of time in jobs, in shops, in shared residences, and so forth, do not enhance their socialization.

There are advantages and disadvantages, for both individuals and collective order and activity, that flow from the fact that the socialization and enculturation of people occur by means of two kinds of mental activity that involve different degrees of awareness.

Behavior based on sub-conceptual modification is dependable, predictable and useful, both to individuals and to the maintenance of collective order. Individual life cannot be lived by paying attention to every item in it any more than a person can drive a car competently as long as every button and pedal is experienced as a separate item to contend with. Collective action cannot occur on the basis of daily improvisation and reorganization. When stability of relationships and performance is important, socialization and enculturation by conditioning and imprinting are an asset. It is a liability when change is desirable or when individuals are required to live in significantly new social circumstances. When this occurs, recourse to conceptual thought and deliberate learning is required for effective adaptation.

It is far easier to make additions to the cultural resources and social skills of individuals, if they do not oppose or contradict previous socialization and enculturation, than to change them. The cultivation of a layman into a professional man is far less difficult, and less distressing to the individual, than the transformations that would be required in the same person if he emigrated to a new society. The association of anxiety with social development makes this so. Since it is anxiety that steers people away from different social and cultural ventures and deflects attention away from the fact that many of the most treasured beliefs and convictions by which they live are arbitrary inventions that they were coerced to integrate in the first place, anything that compels attention to these facts and requires behavior that runs counter to what they acquired when young is likely to release massive anxiety in them.

Since anxiety is among the more uncomfortable states of being, people retreat from it and so they resist conspicuous social and cultural change. Anxiety also interferes with judgment and efficient head work, and so it impedes adaptation to what is new and different. As every teacher can observe, learning is deflected by anxiety if the subject runs counter to religious belief, for example. As psychotherapists and anyone who has undergone therapy knows, anxiety is the chief impediment to improvement in the ability of patients to cope with their social and cultural problems. Unless and until their anxiety is reduced to bearable levels, they are unable to use their knowledge and mental skills to modify their behavior even when these are of high caliber. This is not less true for people who are confronted with major social and cultural changes who, fortunately for them, are free enough of psychiatric pathologies to manage without benefit of professional assistance, or, at least, who try to.

A frequent effect of the anxiety evoked in an individual when some personal trait that is the result of socialization and enculturation is brought into question, or in many people in a population when a reformer or critic applies deliberate analysis to some established social arrangement, such as the authority of monarchs in the seventeenth century, or to cultural formulations such as religious doctrine, is to arouse passionate defense on their behalf, at least initially. This is a widespread phenomenon today for populations around the globe.

New techniques of transportation and communication are probably as responsible as any other one factor. Isolation of populations has broken down and the juxtaposition of the different norms, values, standards of living, etc., of people has evoked attention to much that was long unknown or unnoticed by many of them. The degree of consensus regarding values, institutions, *et al.*, that made for stable social order has been destroyed in more societies than not. Civil war and civil disorders are widespread in which one side defends the status quo against demands for radical changes by the other. One hears pleas and demands for new formulations that will "win the minds of men" and so provide the consensus necessary to ensure cooperation between them. There is every reason to assume that a higher degree of cultural consensus is badly needed. But there is no reason to assume that it can be legislated. It must be cultivated. If current disorders do not lead to the destruction of mankind, new patterns, probably better adapted to the significantly new conditions in the world, will probably emerge. Legislation and exhortations can contribute to this emergence, but the socialization and enculturation of individuals takes time and the modification of the previous socialization and enculturation of adults is difficult and disturbing.

To quote Lorenz: "Demolishing carefully erected structures, though indispensable if better adapted ones are to arise, is always followed by a period of dangerous vulnerability."[3] He is referring to periods of dramatic growth in animals. Sullivan made the same observations about individual human beings and cited the special opportunities for growth or regression in infancy and at the inception of early childhood, adolescence, and the stage when organic regressive changes begin to be conspicuous. The same danger threatens populations as well. Loss of religious faith, doubt regarding political assumptions, uncertainty about economic practices or morals, etc., make people unsure about their behavior in recurring social contexts for which responses were once routine. Needs previously satisfied, though partially, are often no longer satisfied at all. Dissatisfaction and dis-ease prevail until new ways become established as routine ways by means that are for the most part unpredictable and unnoticed.

Because social order and stable relationships depend on a large measure of socialization and enculturation by conditioning and imprinting, the maintenance of order in societies and other large organizations by deliberate, planned,

---

[3] Lorenz, *op. cit., On Aggression.*

rational means is difficult at best. This is one of the reasons for social unrest in industrial societies in which planned obsolescence and change are conspicuous. Rule by law[4] is far more difficult than rule by custom. Both deliberate change and law generally depend upon the threat of external coercions, including force. It takes high levels of self-regulation and cultivated conceptual abilities in people for voluntary compliance from them to be assured. Adults in the societies that rely on planning must have run what they acquired when young through the processes of thought and so freed themselves from anxiety-enforced attachment to the past, if they are to tolerate frequent changes in basic arrangements for living. They must be responsible in their relations with others, if they are to be able to abide by laws without imminent threat of coercion.

Neither of these developments are manifest by the majority of large populations. Therefore, legislation that involves radical changes in relationships between citizens, or in the nature of ownership, and so forth, and the dissemination of verified and tested information via schools and media .of communication, have a disappointingly small effect on the behavior of large numbers of people. Medical knowledge and skills, for example, are still matched by magical practices and backed by traditional beliefs, even in New York, London, and Paris. The enforcement of law, deliberate enactments designed to transcend local mores and create order in large populations, requires police and armies to assure its operation. Civil rights legislation in the United States, or legislation regarding caste relationships in India, vividly illustrate the difficulties.

Nevertheless, as the cultural accumulation increases at accelerating speeds; as societies become large, heterogeneous, secular, mechanized and industrial; as techniques of transportation and communication increase geographic mobility; change by deliberate planning and the maintenance of social order by rational means become necessary for more and more people. It is the chief advantage of human beings

---

[4] Compare William G. Sumner, *op. cit.*, *Folkways*. His distinction between folkways, mores and laws is in part based upon the degree of awareness accorded them that is associated with their mode of transmission.

that they can analyze themselves and the conditions in which they live, that they can regulate their biological impulses and evaluate the results of their own social development. They can lose what might be called "cultural innocence" and be released from automatic responses. They can be socialized and enculturated by conceptual formulation as well as by conditioning and imprinting.

It is this alternative that expands the range of possible human experience and, by enabling people to adapt to increasingly complex social and cultural arrangements, makes it possible for them to realize more and more of their own potentialities. Like other animals, human beings cannot transcend their given potentialities, but these are much greater than those of other animals, and many are still unknown. Like other animals, the innate resources of human beings can be amplified by experience. Unlike other animals, human conceptual abilities enable human beings to create, invent, and improvise as no other creatures can. This gives them the power to investigate rationally the universe in which they live, and themselves. It makes durable associations possible between people who are neither kith nor kin. It may be that in the contemporary state of the world, human survival depends upon the expansion of the social development of the majority of them by conceptual formulation.

In any case, the social development of human beings involves three major sets of factors: their psychobiological resources, their socialization, and their enculturation. These do not exist separately, but they are not merely parts of a single series of processes. Each set of factors appears to have its own potential range of possible cultivation the upper limits of which are only partially known. The distinguishing characteristics of physical maturity have been quite well delineated, those of psychological maturity are still uncertain. The limits of socialization have been roughly determined, those of enculturation are scarcely envisaged. I doubt that it is appropriate to speak of mature enculturation at all. "Adequate" is a more suitable description. But there is little doubt that these developments are manifest in individuals in varying degrees. The extent to which they are, and their combination, determines the level of social development of each individual.

No human being can reach adult competence unless his organism is socialized and enculturated. This is a species requirement, despite the fact that each individual resists the limitation on somatic impulses and satisfactions that social development involves. However, because each human organism provides relatively little of what is required for its social development, the achievement of human maturity is highly problematic and many individuals complete their life span without reaching it.

As a consequence of the dependence of social development on so many factors and conditions that are beyond the direct control of each individual, human beings can be overdeveloped socially, as well as underdeveloped. Because socialization and enculturation always elaborate the conditions that lie between need and satisfaction and modify organic structure and function, it sometimes happens that access to satisfactions is so complicated that the satisfactions are never achieved. If they are vital, people can die from excessive social and cultural interference with their organisms. For example, people in India have died of starvation while cattle roamed around them because cows have been made inedible for them by their enculturation. Serious malfunction of sexual structures and processes are common in individuals who live in populations that support extensive cultural elaborations of sexual functions and provide few social relationships for legitimate sexual satisfaction. The social and cultural modifications of organic systems and the anxiety that has accompanied them are the basis for what is called "psycho-somatic" illness.

On the other hand, if populations are underdeveloped socially, which means that not enough of the people who constitute them are adequately socialized and enculturated, the network of relationships between them and the institutional arrangements that make up a society will begin to fragment and disappear. If the core of cultural consensus necessary for the amount of cooperation needed to sustain societies and the individuals in them diminishes excessively, civil strife is inescapable. If enough people do not master the technical skills that are needed to maintain social order and populations, the order will dissolve and the people will live on a subsistence level at best.

One of the oldest sociological questions is: "What is the relation of individuals to their societies?" and it is appropriate to add, "to their cultures." This book is a partial answer. The psychobiological nature of human beings compels them to live in stable relationships with one another without supplying precise, genetic guarantees for so doing. But the psychobiological resources of individuals do tend to evoke a particular series of relationships for each individual that, in turn, cultivates abilities for more complicated ones. Human mental and linguistic abilities are the ultimate source of what we call culture and have, in turn, come to require the inclusion of large numbers of cultural items in the structures involved to initiate their more mature functions. Large organizations and societies emerge as the number of human beings living in interdependence increases and the cultural store they create and preserve accumulates. These in turn modify the people who participate in them. The social development of individuals depends upon the organizations and culture in which they evolve. The organizations and culture depend upon the social development of the individuals who constitute and use them. The socialization and enculturation of individuals simultaneously lead to their maturity and enable them to operate as the effective social units that initiate and sustain social organizations and culture.

Neither human beings as persons, nor social organizations, nor culture have an independent existence, although they have distinguishing characteristics and properties. What they have in common is absolute dependence on human mental functions. It was the evolutionary development of human conceptual ability that brought these phenomena into existence. They would disappear if human organisms as we know them disappeared. Social science will be greatly advanced when the mystery of human "minds" is solved, not because persons, social organizations, or culture can be reduced to whatever mental activity turns out to be, but because it should reveal the nature of the relations between them. In the meantime, we are limited to identifying and describing some of the ways in which they influence one another and some of their consequences for collective human life.

Bibliographical Background

It is impossible to list all the sources that have gone into a book that summarizes in part the work of thirty years. Though the synthesis is my own, I could probably footnote every paragraph if I could achieve total recall. The best I can do is to present my intellectual forebears.

I grew up in a medical environment and acquired from it an interest in human biology. Academically, I completed two years of medical school. My special, and very amateur interests have been in evolution, embryology, comparative zoology, and general aspects of growth. Therefore, the following books are among those that contributed to my thoughts.

Banton, Michael and Bronowski, J. eds. *Darwinism and the Study of Society.* Chicago: Quadrangle Books, 1961.

Dobzhansky, Theodosius. *Mankind Evolving.* New Haven: Yale University Press, 1962.

Dubois, Rene. "Humanistic Biology," in *The American Scholar,* Spring, 1965.

Huxley, Julian. *Evolution in Action.* New York: Harper, 1952.

————. *Man in the Modern World.* New York: Mentor Books, 1948.

————. *On Living in a Revolution.* New York: Harper, 1944.

Lorenz, Konrad. *On Aggression.* New York: Harcourt Brace, 1963.

————. *King Solomon's Ring.*

Schaller, George B. *The Year of the Gorilla.* Chicago: University of Chicago Press, 1964.

Simeons, A. T. *Man's Presumptuous Brain.* New York: Dutton & Co., 1962.

Simpson, George G. *The Meaning of Evolution.* New Haven: Yale Press, 1949.

Sinnott, Edmund. *The Biology of the Spirit.* New York: Viking Press, 1955.

Whyte, Launcelot Law. *The Unitary Principle in Physics and Biology.* New York: Holt, 1949.

Wiener, Norbert. *The Human Use of Human Beings*. Boston: Houghton Mifflin, 1950.

————. *Cybernetics*. New York: John Wiley, 1948.

Williams, Leonard. *Man and Monkey*. New York: Lippincott, 1968.

My involvement with psychology and psychiatry actually grew out of my experience as an undergraduate in the Sociology-Anthropology Department at the University of Chicago, 1924-1928. This was a period of remarkable ferment in the social sciences, largely stimulated by psychoanalysis and its subsequent application to the social science disciplines. Whatever fallacies this engendered, it initiated the interdisciplinary approach to social science that led to a kind of crossfertilization that has been fruitful in the long run. George Mead was a towering influence on the Sociology-Anthropology Department in those years.

In the early thirties I attended a course on "Personality and Culture" given by Edward Sapir, which was one of the first of its kind. About 1932 I became a member of Lionel Blitzsten's seminar and clinic at Northwestern Medical School, which was a milestone in the development of what has come to be called "dynamic psychiatry." This went on for years. Of all the literature that I have read while following these interests perhaps the following has influenced me most.

Cooley, Charles Horton. *Human Nature and the Social Order*. New York: Scribners, 1902.

Freud, Sigmund. *Collected Papers*. London: Hogarth Press, 1950.

Mead, George. *Mind, Self, and Society*. Chicago: University of Chicago Press, 1946.

Meyer, Adolf. *The Commonsense Psychiatry of Adolf Meyer*. Ed. by Alfred Lief. New York: McGraw-Hill, 1948.

Piaget, Jean. *The Origins of Intelligence in Children*. New York: Norton, 1963.

————. *The Language and Thought of the Child*. New York: World Publishing, 1955.

————. *The Moral Judgment of the Child*. Glencoe, Illinois: Free Press, 1932.

————. *Six Psychological Studies*. New York: Random House, 1967.

Sullivan, Harry Stack. *Conceptions of Modern Psychiatry*. Reprinted from *Psychiatry*, Vol. 3, No. 1 (February, 1940) and Vol. 8, No. 2 (May, 1945).

————. *The Interpersonal Theory of Psychiatry*. New York: Norton, 1953.

————. *The Psychiatric Interview*. New York: Norton, 1954.

————. *Clinical Studies in Psychiatry*. New York: Norton, 1956.
————. *Schizophrenia as a Human Process*. New York: Norton, 1962.
————. *The Fusion of Psychiatry and Social Science*. New York: Norton, 1964.

My major field of specialization as an undergraduate was Sociology-Anthropology. My doctorate from Columbia University in 1952 was in Sociology. Thus it is obvious that I have read the literature that this required. What is relevant here are the people whose works directly influenced me.

Benedict, Ruth. *Patterns of Culture*. New York: Penguin Books, 1946.
Cooley, Charles Horton. *Social Organization*. New York: Schocken Books, 1962.
Durkheim, Emile. *Division of Labor in Society*. Trans. by George Simpson. Glencoe, Illinois: Free Press, 1949.
————. *Suicide*. Trans. by John Spaulding and George Simpson. Glencoe, Illinois: Free Press, 1951.
Lippman, Walter. *Public Opinion*. New York: Macmillan Co., 1956.
Park, Robert Ezra. *Society*. Glencoe, Illinois: Free Press, 1955.
————. *Human Communities*. Glencoe, Illinois: Free Press, 1952.
Robinson, James Harvey. *The Mind in the Making*. New York: Harpers, 1921.
Sapir, Edward. *Selected Writings of Edward Sapir*. Ed. by David G. Mandelbaum. Berkeley: University of California Press, 1949.
Simmel, Georg. *The Sociology of Georg Simmel*. Trans. by Kurt Wolff. Glencoe, Illinois: The Free Press, 1950.
Spykman, Nicholas. *The Social Theory of Georg Simmel*. New York: Atherton Press, 1966.
Tocqueville, Alexis de. *Democracy in America*. Two volumes. New York: Vintage Books, 1954.
Veblen, Thorstein. *The Theory of the Leisure Class*. New York: Random House, 1931.
Weber, Max. *Max Weber: Essays in Sociology*. Trans. and ed. by H. H. Gerth and C. Wright Mills. New York: Oxford University Press, 1946.
————. *Max Weber: The Theory of Social and Economic Organization*. Trans. by A. M. Henderson and Talcott Parsons. New York: Oxford University Press, 1947.
————. *The Protestant Ethic and the Spirit of Capitalism*. Trans. by Talcott Parsons. New York: Scribner, 1930.

Index

Abilities, appearance of, 48; adolescent, 107-9

Abstract conceptualization, preadolescent, 87 ff

Abstract thought, adolescent, 107 ff

Adaptation to groups, children's, 60 ff

Adolescence, physiological change in, 101 ff; from pre-adolescence, 100

Adolescent impact on society, 122-24

Adolescents vs. young adults, 141

Adult society and adolescents, 122-24

Adults, children and, 58; and juveniles, 70-71, 73 ff

Aging, adaptation to, 157 ff

Altruism, 21

Anxiety, 32, 33 ff, 38-39, 62 ff; juvenile, 82-83; middle age, 149-50; sex and, in adolescence, 101 ff, 112 ff; in middle age, 144-45; social maturity and, 138; uncertainty and, in adolescence, 119-20

Approval, peer, juvenile need of, 82-83

Approval—disapproval, 34 ff

Arrested social capacities, 66-67

Association, conceptual, children's, 54 ff

Associations, juvenile, see Teams and team life

Athletic teams, juvenile, see Teams and team life

Authority and juveniles, 71 ff, 83

Authority and leadership, 85

"Autistic" conceptualization, 51

Autoeroticism, adolescent, 121-22

Autonomy, juvenile, lack in peer groups, 74

Awareness and maturity, 125 ff

"Batignolles, The," 97

Biological growth, 46-47

Change, resistance to, 149-50

Change and social order, 134 ff

Change of attitudes, children's, 61 ff

Change of culture, effect of, 65-67

Childhood, psychobiological resources, 49

Children into juveniles, 67-68 ff

Children vs. children, 58

Choice as juvenile alternative, 71

"Codes," juvenile, 82

Coercion, 35 ff, 42-44, 46; of adolescent sex impulses, 103-4; of adolescents, 117-19

Collaboration, among adults, 139; and friendship, 94-95

Colonialism as a source of dependence, 22

Community leadership, 85

Community organizations, adult, 146

Competence, juvenile, 73 ff; middle age, 150

Competition, athletic, 75 ff

Competition among juveniles, 79 ff; among adults, 139-40

Competition and cooperation, juvenile, 79-81

Compromise, children and, 64

"Conceptual realism" (Piaget), 51

Conceptualization, children's, 50 ff; juvenile, 69-70, 91; preadolescent, 87 ff; adolescent, 106 ff

Conservatism, adolescents', 115; middle age, 148-50

Cooley, Charles, cited, 95 ff

Cooperation, children and, 64

Cooperation and competition, juvenile, 79-81

Cooperation in adult societies, 131 ff, 139

Cooperation, team, 75 ff

Coordination, physical, in children, 49

Crying, 40-41, 46-47

Cultural growth, pre-adolescent, 92-93

Cultural requisitions, 24

Death of the aged, 157, 160

Defiance, adolescent, 118

Dependency, personal, in society, 132-33

Dependency or relationships, 58 ff

Deviation, sexual, adolescent, 121-22

Differences, biological, 15 ff; cultural, 15 ff; mental, 16 ff

Don Juan complex, 121

Education, formal, and juveniles, 78

Egalitarianism among adults, 140-41

Egocentricicity, 64-65, 88; adolescent, 109

Elders, responsibility for, 145-46

Empathy, 32-33; vs. sympathy, 93-94

Enculturation, 192-203

Equality, interpersonal, 138

Eroticism, adolescent, 121-22

"Establishment, The," 118

Ethnocentrism, social, 148

Family-adolescent relations, values, 119-20

Family concept, children's, 56-57

Family groups vs. peer groups, 71 ff

Family life, young adult, 134

Fear 33

Foresight, young adult capacities, 128 ff

Folkways, 54 ff

Freudianism, 28-29, 102-3

Friendship, the mark of pre-adolescence, 84-85, 86 ff; and collaboration, 94-95; and sympathy, 93

Fromm, Erich, cited, 67

Frustration, sexual, origins, 102 ff

Gangs, see Groups

Generation gap, 73 ff, 97-100, 110 ff, 113-15, 145, 159

Group adaptation, children's, 60 ff

Group participation, children's, 57-58; juveniles', 81 ff
Groups, juvenile 70; adult, 97-98
Growth, cultural, pre-adolescent, 92-93
Growth, social, 16 ff, 66-67

Habits, children's, 61 ff
Handicapped children, 49
"Head Start," 55
Hesse, Hermann, cited, 93n
Homosexuality, 121-22
Hostility, adolescent, 111 ff

"Ideal" as a concept, 28
Idealism, frustrated, and adolescents, 113
Illiteracy, 129-30
Imaginativeness, adolescents and, 128 ff
Infancy, biological needs and resources, 30-31; psychological conditions in, 39-40
Infants into children, 46-47 ff
Integration, racial and religious, 37-38
Interpersonal relationships, young adult, 130-34
"Intrinsic" worth, recognition by pre-adolescents, 95-100
Isolation, social, among aged, 159 ff

Language, 52-53; juvenile, 70; adolescent, 106 ff
"Latency" and "potential" contrasted, 17-19
Laws, compliance with, 117 ff
Leader authority, 85
Leadership, juvenile, 71
Learning process and pre-adolescents, 93
Leisure, 136 ff

Libido, 58, 59
Linguistic maturity, 129 ff
Littwak, Edward, cited, 22
Loneliness, friendship and, 91
Lorenz, Konrad, quoted, 194, 201-2, 202-3, 204, 211
Lust, 38, 105

Male-female relationships, old age, 155 ff
Malinowsky, Bronislaw, cited, 57
Manners, 54 ff
Mating as adolescent goal, 110, 118-19
Maturity, social, 125 ff
Mead, George, cited, 94
Mental abilities, 16 ff
Mentors vs. teachers, 93
Middle age, 142-51
Mores, social, 54 ff
Mothering, 41 ff

Occupations, see Skills
"Oedipal phase," 57; theory, 112
Old age, 150-63
Operation Head Start, 55
Organizational leadership, 85
Organizations, adult, 146
Ostracism, 79, 81

Pain, 33-34
"Parataxic" conceptualization, 51
Parent-adolescent relations, values, 110 ff, 119-20
Parents, middle-aged, 145
Peer groups, children's, 58; juvenile, 69 ff, 72 ff, 77 ff; lack of autonomy, 74; adolescent values, 107 ff, 113; peer groups vs. peers, 71 ff
Personality changes, 29
Physiological change, adolescent, effects, 104-5

Physiological stability, juvenile, 69

Piaget, Jean, cited, 82; quoted, 108-9, 122-23

"Potential," definition, 17-19

Pre-adolescence to adolescence, 100

Prestige and adulthood, 146

Punishment, see Anxiety

Quixotism of adolescents, 128 ff

Relationships, children's, 58 ff; young adults, 130-34

Reliability, individual, 26

Resentment, adolescent, 111 ff

Responsibility, individual, 26

Retirement, problems of, 143-44; old age, 153 ff

Riesman, David, cited, 82

Role-playing and social competence, 92-93

Satisfaction, infants' response, 31; as mark of friendship, 89-91

Satisfaction in giving satisfaction, 125 ff

Satisfactions of maturity, 125 ff

Self-consciousness, adolescent, 115

Self-esteem, requisites for, 91-92

Self-regulation, 21

Sex differentiation, adolescent, 109

Sex impulses, coercion, 103-4

Sex in adolescence, 101 ff

Sexual anxiety, middle age, 144-45

Sexual attraction, adolescent, 118-19, 121-22

Sexual frustration, origins, 102 ff; adolescent resentment, 111 ff

Sexual satisfaction, adolescent, 105-6

Sexuality, old age, 155 ff

Sibling competition, 79

Simeons, A. T. W., cited, 129

Simmel, Georg, cited, 60

Skills, occupational, young adult, 134

Social animal, the, 15

Social development, origins, 13 ff; purpose, 14; growth, 16 ff; stages, 19, 27, 48

Social life, foundation, 204-15

Social maturity, 20, 125 ff Social order, 134 ff

Social relationships, interpersonal, 25 ff

Social skills, 48; pre-adolescent, 98-100

Socialization, 164-91

Societal impact of adolescents, 122-24

Sociophysiological changes in adolescence, 101 ff

Sound in infancy, 47

Speech, in infancy, 47; children's, 49 ff, 55

Stability, juvenile physiological, 69; social, 134 ff

"Stages of development," 19, 27, 48

Strangers (nonfamilial) and adolescents, 114-15

Subordination, infant, 44-45; among adults, 140-41

Sullivan, Harry Stack, cited, 86 passim

Superordination, infant 44-45; among adults, 140-41

Symbols, children and, 50

Sympathy vs. empathy, 93-94

Teams and team life, 75 ff
Tenderness, 43-44
Tolerance, 81, 92, 107, 147-48
"Typical" as a concept, 28

Ward, Lester, cited, 137
Wisdom of the aged, 158
Women in old age, 155 ff
Written language, 53

Vocabulary, 52
Voluntary service, adult, 146

Young adults, 121, 126-42; vs.
    adolescents, 141